I'M JUST THAT INTO

ME :)

YOU'RE THE ONE
YOU'VE BEEN WAITING FOR

DAYNA MASON

&

JASON ANDRADA

Printed in the United States of America
First Printing: Sept 2017

International Standard Book Number-13:
  9780997893823   (Softcover)
International Standard Book Number-10:
  0997893826   (Softcover)

Published by Seattle Indie Press, Kent, WA
www.SeattleIndiePress.com

Visit the authors' websites at:

www.DaynaMasonAuthor.com
www.JasonAndrada.com

Facebook: www.facebook.com/ImJustThatIntoMe/

Dear Reader,

Are you tired of ending up in dysfunctional relationships or do you avoid them altogether because it's easier that way? Could there be buried events in your past that may be contributing? Would you like to be truly happy regardless of your relationship status or current circumstances? Then this book is for you.

Both of us experienced a traumatic, life-altering event when we were young, which changed and defined each of our lives in significantly damaging ways. Our inability to see the truth about the incidents left us disconnected from any real relationship, and the relationships we did have were detrimental to our wellbeing.

This is not a traditional "self-help" book. The stories in this book, based on our real lives, are intended to take you on a quest that affects your behavior going forward, similar to the way the well-known fable, "The Boy Who Cried Wolf," shifts the reader's viewpoint by demonstrating the disadvantages of lying.

We are confident that through reading our stories and doing your own self-discovery using the practical tools at the end of this book, you'll learn a different way of being in the world and in relationships, which will change your perspective and your choices in the future.

- Dayna (aka "Anne") & Jason (aka "Dominic")

✿ ANNE

The Mess

Regret flows through my body and seeps out through the gash in my hand, splattering crimson onto the crisp autumn leaves at my feet.

Is this what my life has come to? I'm an idiot. I look at Derek through the eight-foot tall wire fence that separates us.

"Oh, *hell*, no," he declares, staring at my hands as I attempt to control the bleeding with a clump of leaves. "I'm going around." He disappears around the corner of the building.

What? He made me climb this stupid fence because he didn't want to wait in line to get back into the bar, and now *he's going around*?

I'm pathetic. Why do I desperately want to be with someone who doesn't seem to care about me?

I see the pain in his heart. I see how he struggles, and I want to love the rough edges off. I'm a rescuer. That's what they call people like me, who value love and relationships above all else. He just needs to learn how to love himself first, I rationalize. Then he'll be able to love me.

I've been told loving him is not the problem, the issue is losing myself in the process. I know it's not healthy, but I can't stop myself. Every time I grow too weary and want to walk away, hope takes me hostage again.

I glance at my palm in the dim light of the one bulb that hasn't burned out above the bar's back entrance. A pool of blood is welling up where moments ago I had frantically clutched at the barbed wire to keep from plummeting to the ground. How bad is it? I head toward the back door of the club and make my way to the restroom.

I toss the leaves in the garbage and examine my hand closely.

"Oh, my God! What happened?" A blonde twenty-something girl with bright red lipstick and five-inch heels is gawking at me.

"I cut myself." I turn towards the paper towel dispenser and attempt to fashion a makeshift bandage.

"Damn, that's nasty," she says.

I wanna say, "No shit," but my frustration would be misplaced.

She glances at her reflection in the mirror one last time and, satisfied, heads out the door.

I can't believe I agreed to climb that fence. I care more about making him happy than about cutting my fucking hand off. What the hell is wrong with me? I finish wrapping my hand and follow the blonde out the door.

The blare of the distorted music annoys me and the pulsating lights are not illuminating enough to scan the room for Derek. I approach the bar and spot him at the front door, showing his ID. We make eye contact but he doesn't care enough to look at my hand.

"I need a drink," he yells over the music as he passes by me.

Asshole. Don't you see that I'm bleeding to death?

Despite my anger, I follow him to the bar. He hands me a glass of wine and walks towards the stage.

I finish my fourth drink in the last hour and return to the restroom. I wrap fresh paper towels around my hand. The bleeding has almost stopped. Not that I care. The alcohol has drowned my give-a-shit gene.

I stagger over to Derek in the back of the crowd near the stage. I hate him for not even asking if I'm alright.

I want to tell him what a jerk he is, but I know this feeling will fade, like it always does, and again I'll look for ways to please him and not be a burden.

"This sucks. Let's go." He walks towards the front entrance to the club.

Trent And Derek

Moonlight casts shadows into Derek's bedroom through the French doors. The body next to me is snoring. Oh yeah, I must've passed out after we had sex. I struggle to remember the details of the night. Derek took care of my hand. That's right, when we got back to his house, he put antiseptic on it and wrapped it in gauze. He loves me. I feel the smile creep across my face in the dark.

My hand. I touch my palm where the pain is located. It's swollen and the wrap is saturated. I crawl out of bed and tiptoe to the bathroom.

Oh my God. My hand is a mess. There's a large, deep groove in my palm, exposing pink flesh in the valley where it's split. I need stitches.

I don't want to wake Derek, but I have to get this taken care of.

"Derek." I gently nudge his shoulder.
"Huh. What?"
"I think I need stitches. My hand is really bad."

5

"No, you don't. You're fine."

"No, seriously. It's swelling. I think it's infected."

"Okay." He rolls over and drifts back to sleep.

"Derek, can I use your car to go to the hospital?"

"Huh? Yeah, go ahead." He mutters and drifts off again.

I find an out-of-the-way place to sit in the emergency room of the University of Washington Medical Center, the closest hospital to Derek's Queen Anne hill home that I could think of. It's 8:03 a.m. on my phone. Derek will probably still be sleeping when I return. I hate not being able to come and go as I please. I'd have my car with me if I hadn't agreed to let Derek pick me up at my apartment on Capitol Hill. But I couldn't resist a ride in the Lamborghini his dealership recently acquired. Even though he deals in *luxury* vehicles, he's still just a stereotypical used-car salesman. Sometimes I can barely tolerate listening to his feigned interest on the phone with his clients, knowing that as soon as he hangs up, he's going to tell me all about what idiots they are, because he thinks most people are idiots.

I keep ending up in relationships with jerks who are unavailable. Whether they're pining over some ex-girlfriend, or longing for some girl who doesn't want them, or not ready for a relationship, or in Derek's case, never want to be in a committed relationship again because his ex-wife broke his heart, it's all the same. Unavailable. Oh sure, they'll have sex with me and even be in a relationship with me, but no matter who it is, they're never fully in it.

After decades of analyzing myself and hundreds of self-help books, not much has changed. Here I sit, alone, in the ER, even though I *have a boyfriend.*

I would never let *him* go to the hospital alone. I would be there, by his side, every step of the way. So why do I make it okay for him to not be here for me?

A tall man with sandy-brown hair, a husky build and a boyish face sits across from me. He's not someone I would normally find attractive, but there's something about him that grabs my attention.

He smiles at me.

I smile back.

"Hi. What've ya got there?" I point to the large plastic-covered frames that are leaning against the bench next to him.

"A couple of art pieces I'm donating to the hospital."

"Can I see them?"

"Sure." He pulls the clear covering off each canvas and supports them side by side for me to view.

They're gorgeous. Vibrant colors on canvas. A blend of paint, paper, cloth and possibly metal? I've never seen anything like it.

"Wow, those are amazing. Where'd you get them?"

"I made them. I work primarily in mixed-media. That's a combination of different—"

"I know!" My enthusiasm gets the best of me. I knew there was something special about him. Of course there is, he's an artist. I've always treasured creative expression in all its forms. As a child, I remember being emotionally moved by the words in books and wanting to be an author who changes lives when I grew up. But growing up in poverty has a way of persuading you to do the practical. So, instead of pursuing the life of a starving artist, I got a business degree, climbed the corporate ladder like a good little minion and joined the ranks of the Chief Executive Officer community. At age 35, I enjoy the recognition for successful direction of a large financial corporation, but I rarely see my beautiful apartment and I feel less fulfilled than I ever imagined.

"I'm Anne. What's your name?"

"Trent." He extends his hand. "So, are you an artist?" His slightly-raised eyebrow and dimpled smile are adorable.

"No, but I love art and my company has been looking for new mixed-media pieces for our building in Bellevue. I'd love to connect you with our buyer."

"Well, thank you, Anne," Trent says. "Ya know, maybe our paths have crossed for a reason."

I feel it, too, like our meeting has been divinely orchestrated.

"I think you may be right about that." I look directly into his eyes, green, like the color of seafoam. They say the eyes are the windows to the soul. I don't know who *they* are, but I do think there's some truth to that. He's handsome, not like a hunk, more like a classic gentleman.

"What happened to your hand?" He's staring at my bandage.

"Oh, yeah, I think I need stitches. That's why I'm here."

"How'd that happen?" His voice is comforting and the gentle concern on his face compels me to tell him more than I probably should.

"It was stupid. I drunkenly climbed a barbed-wire fence. It was my boyfriend's idea, and then after he saw my hand, no surprise, he changed his mind."

"What? Why were you climbing the fence?"

"Well, that's the really dumb part. We were at a bar and we went outside so he could smoke a cigarette. When he finished, there was a line to get back in and he didn't want to wait. So, I followed him to the back of the building, where there was an eight-foot fence and he told me to go first, that this was how we were getting back into the club. I was terrified. I told him no way, but he insisted and made fun of me for hesitating. So, I climbed the fence."

"He sounds like a jerk." Trent's face looks protective, like a big brother who's plotting to kick some ass.

"It's my own fault for going along with it."

"That may be true, but it's his responsibility as a man to protect you. Not to put you in harm's way," Trent says authoritatively. "He's not a man. He's a jerk. Sorry, but I don't like him. Where is he now? Why isn't he here with you?"

I should've kept my big mouth shut.

"Um, he was sleeping and I didn't want to wake him, so I drove myself." It's sorta true, he was sleeping.

"I'm sorry I got so upset, it's none of my business. I just hate it when guys treat women poorly. It's not right."

Trent leans back in his chair.

"That's okay."

9

"Trent Jack?" says a woman in a lab coat as she approaches us. "I'm Doctor Casey."

Trent Jack? What a horrible name. Poor guy.

"That's me." He grabs his art, stands up and looks in my direction.

"It was a pleasure meeting you, Anne. Please take care of yourself." He reaches into his coat pocket. "Here's my card. Let's get together sometime. Give me a call, okay?"

"I will. Thanks."

As I watch Trent walk away, I feel like something important just happened.

I try not to wake Derek as I crawl back into bed. I can't believe I needed five stitches. Well, at least they used the dissolvable kind, so I don't have to go back to the hospital and have them removed.

I can't stop thinking about what Trent said. Is Derek really a jerk? Is it the man's responsibility to protect me? That's just old-fashioned nonsense. Women are empowered to be independent. I don't need a man to take care of me. I can take care of myself. But I want to feel safe in his arms. I crave it. Hmm.

Derek rolls over. He squints his eyes at me as he adjusts to the daylight coming in through the window.

"Where'd ya go, baby doll?"

"Don't you remember? I went to the hospital. I got stitches." I show him my bandaged hand.

"Oh yeah. Come here." He reaches around my waist and pulls me against his warm body. I wish he wanted to hold me, look me in the eyes, and tell me how much he loves me. But romance isn't his thing.

He tugs at my pants and rolls on top of me.

"Tell me you want me," he commands.

Ugh. I hate talking during sex.

"I want you."

"Like you mean it." I feel his arms tense up around me.

I hate it when he's aggressive. I want to make love … I don't want it like this. Oh, stop it, Anne. Grow up. Do you want him to think you're no fun?

"I. Want. You." I take a deep breath. *Please believe me.*

"That's better," he says, pleased with my compliance.

I'm gone. I move my body at the right times and in the right ways to keep up the charade, but I'm no longer there. I retreat to my familiar place of numbness where everything is fine—that place where what's happening has no power.

The clanging of pans echoes from the kitchen.

"Whatcha doin'?" I'm hungry. I hope he's making something yummy.

"I'm making you blueberry pancakes, baby."

Aw, sometimes he can be so sweet. Why can't he be like this all the time?

I peek around the corner into the kitchen and admire his tall, husky, naked-except-for-his-boxer-briefs body as he stands in front of the stove.

"Thank you for making us breakfast, babe."

"Sure. Go, look in the living room." Derek says, and in one sweeping motion, flips the hotcakes in the pan.

I glance around the partial wall that separates the living area from the kitchen and see a large bouquet of red roses in a vase and a Starbucks cup. He must've gotten those while I was sleeping.

"Oh, my gosh! Thank you so much." I hurry over to Derek and attempt to cover his face in kisses.

"It's nothin'. Now, drink your mocha before it gets cold."

I remove a rose from the vase and inhale the fragrance. I take a sip of my favorite coffee drink. It's still warm. It's times like these that give me hope. There are so many things I want to say to him. *I love it when you do things for me, you are adorable standing there in your underwear, I hate it when you are aggressive in bed.* I wish I could tell him how I feel without him making me feel stupid for having feelings.

Washing dishes by hand is relaxing for me. Derek is a germaphobe, so I place each item carefully into the dishwasher in its predefined spot. Dammit, I can't remember where he said the coffee mugs go. I glance over at Derek in his leather office chair. Never mind, I don't want to deal with him taunting me for forgetting. I'll just put the mugs next to the plates and hope he doesn't notice.

I sit down at the long table in the dining room. Derek walks toward the window, cigarette in hand. The smell of his disgusting American Spirit habit is burning my eyes and nose, even with the window open.

The adrenaline floods my body. Just do it, ya big chicken. At work, I can confront any situation with authority and finesse. I give presentations to thousands of people, hire and fire employees, and have tough conversations every day. But, when it comes to my personal life, I struggle with confrontation. Even though the fear of having someone I love upset with me is paralyzing, I need to know if Derek wants a future with me, or if I'm just wasting my time.

"Do you like our relationship?" I wait hesitantly for his answer.

"No, not at all, that's why I never call you or invite you to stay over at my house."

Why does he have to be sarcastic? Ugh. Why can't he just say, *yes, I like our relationship.*

"Do you even like me?"

"I'll never tell you I like you, 'cause that would be the end."

"If you never tell me, then *that* will be the end."

"Whatevah." He takes a drag of his cancer-stick and exhales toward the window.

This is going nowhere. I want out. I'm afraid, though, to have that conversation.

I finish my coffee and go for a walk.

I look out over the city of Seattle, seated on a stone wall in Kerry Park, a few blocks from Derek's house.

Derek cares about me. I'm somewhat sure he loves me. At least as much as he's capable. Is it enough? I wish I could talk to him about things that are important to me. He can be loving and romantic when he wants to be. I just wish it was more often. Are my expectations too high? I've been in a lot of relationships. Maybe it's time for me to just accept that there are no ideal relationships and what I have with Derek is good enough. It's not his fault that I'm afraid to speak up for what I want.

The Trip

The doorman at the hotel places my luggage and Derek's backpack on a cart and directs us to the check-in desk on the second floor. I allow myself to get excited again. We are in New York City! I love the sounds of the honking horns, the traffic, the people, the hustle of the expedited pace of this vibrant urban location that seems to embody its own personality as if it were alive. After two years of dating and one year of hinting to Derek about wanting to join him on his annual trip to New York City, we're finally here. The trip was his idea. I'm trying not to get my hopes up, but he has even suggested several times that I should move in with him. He gave up one of the rooms in his house for me to use as an office when I'm there. Then, out of the blue, he planned this trip to *my* favorite place. The signs are there; he's going to propose.

We check in, and ride the elevator to the fifteenth floor.

"That's bullshit. I've been coming here for years.

They should know me and be kissing my ass." Derek is angry that we were given keys to the room he had reserved instead of being given a complimentary upgrade like he'd been given in years past.

Derek opens the door to the room and I step in behind him.

Wow. The room is large for a New York hotel in the city and it's decorated in patterns of yellow, black and white—the black carpet and stainless steel coffee table add to the metropolitan vibe. Across the room on the other side of the king-size bed is a sliding glass door. A balcony? I walk over to the window and see the small steel grate balcony, which resembles a fire-escape without the ladder and offers a view overlooking a large section of East Village.

"Hey, man, I'm here. Can I meet ya in about fifteen minutes?" I turn to see Derek on his cell phone. Are we going somewhere?

"Okay. See ya," Derek says into the phone.

"I've gotta go somewhere. I'll be back in a half hour," Derek says as he walks toward the door.

"Okay." I know asking questions would only agitate him and he'd say it's none of my business anyway.

I hear the beep from the keycard outside our room. Derek walks in, heads directly to the bathroom, and shuts the door.

"Everything okay?" I call to him through the bathroom door as I hear rustling and shuffling from the other side. What's he doing in there? I'm sure he heard me.

I don't want to make him mad, so I don't ask again.

Geez, it's been thirty minutes. I'm getting hungry. I wonder if we are going to—

The door swings open and Derek walks across the room, hurls his body onto the bed, and gazes upward.

"Are you hungry?" I'm nervous asking, because he seems to be in his own world. I'm not sure what to do.

"No. We'll go to dinner later." He dismisses me and continues to stare at the ceiling.

Later? How much later? How long is he going to lay there? What am I supposed to do in the meantime? I can't ask him. I'll just wait until he's ready.

I pick up my phone from the coffee table and scroll through my Facebook feed.

Derek retrieves the remote from the nightstand and navigates to the Adult category on the TV. He selects the 24-hour option and presses the button to purchase it.

What? Did he forget I'm here? What the heck is he doing?

He turns up the volume and fast-forwards past the current scene.

"I can't stand watching women fake it." He stops at the next scene and examines it for a few minutes. "There, see that, you can tell *she* likes it."

What am I supposed to say? I don't want to watch this, let alone talk about it. What is happening? I thought he wanted me here. Why is he watching *that* and ignoring me?

The scene is over and he is fast-forwarding again. He pauses briefly at the next scene and skips-ahead again. The girl must've been faking it. Whatever. They all look like they're faking it to me.

I can't believe he's been watching porn for over an hour. I'm going to lose my mind.

"I'm going to the lobby for a while. I'll have my phone if you need to reach me." I grab my backpack and make my way towards the door.

"Uh-huh." Derek looks bored but doesn't take his eyes off the screen.

The Lobby

I step off the elevator and pass the check-in desk on my way to the large lobby seating area. There's an empty couch near the wall of windows on the other side of the room. Perfect. I place my backpack on the coffee table and glance outside at the steady stream of people and cars on Rivington Street.

My phone rings. It's my boss.

"Hello?"

"Hi, Anne. It's Don. Sorry to bother you on vacation, but I'm finalizing my presentation to the board and I have a question about next year's budget. Do you have a minute?"

"Sure, Don. Whaddya need?"

"You've included a significant savings in vendor software next year. Can you explain how this is possible?"

"Certainly," I say, as I lean into the stiff, bright yellow and black pillows that decorate the couch. They look better than they feel. "I was able to negotiate substantial savings with our three main vendors by getting extremely competitive quotes from their competition. I had to haggle a bit, but they conceded in order to keep our business." I glance at myself in a silver framed mirror above the end table. Yeah, that's right. I'm a badass.

"Nicely done, Anne." I can hear the smile in his voice. "How's vacation? Are you in New York yet?"

"Yes, I am. Just arrived today. It's great so far." I hate lying, but he doesn't need to know the truth.

"Well, enjoy yourself. We got ya covered here."

"I will. Thanks, Don."

"No problem. Talk to you later."

"Talk to ya later, Don."

I take a deep breath and feel the tension start to leave my shoulders. I scan the room. On the right of the entryway the wall is covered in shelves of books, and to the left is a large bar with what looks like snacks.

I'm starving. I wonder what they've got to offer.

Most of the seating in the room is occupied by well-dressed, business-looking people on their phones or laptops. I reach the counter and survey the array of cookies, apples, bananas, a small plate of cheese and crackers, ice water, and coffee.

I grab a little of everything, which takes me two trips, and settle in to my small corner of heaven in this otherwise hellish experience.

My phone rings. It's Dominic.

"Your spidey-sense working again?" I ask. "How'd ya know I needed to talk to you?"

"Well, let's see." Dominic says. "It could be my spidey-sense or it could be that you traveled to your favorite place with my least favorite person. How is His Highness doing, anyway?" Dominic's such a smart ass, but the comfort of his voice wraps around me like a warm blanket. In the ten years that we've been friends, he's always had a knack for reaching out at just the right time, or saying exactly what I need to hear at the moment I need to hear it.

"So, are you going to be *nice*?" I ask, in my best Mom voice.

"Absolutely. I'll be nice when he's no longer a douche or when you dump him and marry me."

"Marry you? Ew, that's gross. You're like my brother." I feign disgust.

"Brothers and sisters get married sometimes. *Rawr.*" Dominic loves to push the boundaries with his teasing to get a reaction out of people, but I'm no longer surprised by anything he says.

"*Anyway.* You timed that perfectly," I say. "I'm going to believe it was your spidey-sense and ignore the rest of your nonsense. Derek's up in the room and I'm hanging out in the lobby of the hotel. I had to get away from him for a bit."

"Didn't you just get there? What the hell did he do to you already?"

"Oh, nothing. He just wants to lay around the room until dinner and I got bored, so I'm hanging out in the lobby drinking coffee and eating a snack. I thought I could get caught up on some work." I want to tell him the truth, but I know he'll get upset and worry and there's nothing he can do about it anyway.

"Bullshit. I hear it in your voice." He knows me too well. "I'm here for you, even if I have to fly out there and kick his ass. But I need to know why I'm punching him when he asks?"

"No, Dominic. I don't want you to beat up my boyfriend. Thanks for the offer." I know he's only somewhat teasing. "I'll fill you in on the details when I'm back, I don't want to get into it now. But so far, it's not been the trip I'd imagined. It's weird, Derek took off as soon as we got here, then came back an hour later and went straight to the bathroom and stayed in there forever. I've no idea what that was about."

"What's wrong with him? He's on vacation with a beautiful woman and he's ignoring her? I can assure you if it were me, you wouldn't be in the lobby by yourself in your favorite city."

"Aw, thanks, Dominic." Why can't I be attracted to someone like him? Why do I always go for the edgy guys?

"So, guess what happened today? C'mon, c'mon. Guess." Dominic says.

"What? Geez, lay off the caffeine," I tease, but I do love his enthusiasm.

"I've been invited to speak in front of six thousand people at a convention for assault and grief this summer! Can you believe that?" Dominic has helped transform many people's lives with his one-on-one counseling. I've often thought that he could do more with a bigger audience.

"That's awesome, and yes, of course I can believe that. You're different from other counselors. When you work with someone, their life actually changes. It's about time you start getting the recognition you deserve and own your awesomeness." He's come a long way from the insecure man I met years ago, but I still have to remind him sometimes how brilliant he is.

"I am pretty freakin' awesome, aren't I?" I love the confidence in his voice.

"Yes, you are. And it's not cocky to know who you are."

"Thanks, pal."

"Do you know what you'll talk about at the convention?"

"Oh, I don't know, maybe assault and grief?" He says and laughs at his own sarcasm. "I have a few ideas, nothing for sure."

"Do you want me to help you narrow down your choices?" I love to lasso the ambiguous and make it achievable.

"I do, but not yet. Let me think about it first."

"Okay. Just let me know."

"You know I will. Who else can I talk with about these things? You and Josie are my lifelines, and the only people that will put up with me."

"Thanks, Dom." Josie gave him the nickname and I've adopted it over the years. Our affection for each other seems a little unconventional for a friendship. I gave up a long time ago trying to conform to the world's way of seeing things. It leaves no room for love. Real love. Not the creepy I want to get into your pants kind, but the kind that says, I know what you need and I'm here to provide it. I knew within the first year of meeting Dominic, our love for each other was different. It had nothing to do with dating; it had everything to do with seeking to understand each other and the intention to help each other in any way we could to realize our best lives.

"Well, I've gotta run some errands. Are you sure you're okay?" He sounds concerned.

"Yes, I'm better now. Thanks for knowing to call. It really is good to hear your voice."

"I'll talk to ya tomorrow. You call me anytime you need to, okay?"

"I will. Thanks again for caring so much."

"Of course."

Dinner

I check the time on my phone. Wow, it's been three hours. Derek must be ready to get dinner now. I gather my stuff and make my way back to the room. I open the door and there he is, exactly where I left him, lying on the bed, remote in hand. I don't think he's moved since I left. I flop on the couch with my backpack.

"Are we going to dinner soon?"

"Not yet. I've got some things to do first." What on earth could he possibly have to do now? What does that even mean? It's after seven … are we ever going to eat?

"Whaddya need to do?" Maybe if I can help, we can leave sooner.

"Stuff." He moves briskly over to the mini-bar and picks up two cellophane-wrapped water glasses, carries them across the room, and places them on a shelf above the desk. He stares at the desk, then picks up a pen and pad of paper, strides back to the mini-bar and puts them meticulously on a shelf above the snacks. He walks quickly back to the desk and inspects the scene again. He then moves the telephone methodically from one side of the desk to the other, positioning and repositioning it as if it must be at just the right angle. I'm fascinated as he continues to move objects erratically from one location to another, sometimes moving the same object multiple times to new locations.

What's he doing? He grabs the plastic liner from the garbage container and kneels on the floor. He picks something imperceptible out of the carpet, inspects it and places it on his tongue. He inches over to another part of the carpet and picks something else out of the carpet and puts it in the bag. He stands up and snatches the two empty beer bottles on the nightstand for his trash bag, then glances toward me on the couch.

"If you want to go to dinner sooner, you could help clean the room."

Clean the room? What is he talking about? We just got here. The room isn't even messy.

"Won't the maid take care of that?"

He ignores me and continues his bizarre ritual.

"You ready to go?" Derek says.

I look up from my phone. It's now after 8:00 p.m. and he is standing by the door, mysterious garbage in hand.

"Um, yeah, I am." I jump from the couch and hoof it to the door. Is he taking that sack with him?

We exit the hotel and walk to the end of the block.

"There's a trash can." I point to the bin a few feet from where we're standing.

"No, not that one." The traffic signal changes and he walks ahead of me.

What does he mean, *that one?* Does his magical garbage need a special receptacle?

We arrive at a small, seat-yourself Mexican restaurant and find a table. I can't believe he still has that stupid garbage sack with him. We passed at least four trash bins on our way here. What is he waiting for? And he brought it into the restaurant. He's never acted like this before. Maybe New York brings out the crazy in him.

☼

Derek walks into the middle of the four-lane street with his arm outstretched. The first yellow taxi zooms by, then another. The next one slows and pulls to the curb and Derek opens the rear passenger-side door.

"Get in."

I hop into the car and slide over to the driver's side. Derek slides in next to me.

"Meatpacking district." Derek hasn't said much since we arrived. It's almost odd to hear his voice now.

The cab driver starts the meter and glances in his rearview mirror.

"How're you two doing tonight?"

"Fine." There's lightness in Derek's voice, almost like he's starting to enjoy himself.

"Is this your first time in New York?"

"No," I say, "he used to live here and I've been here many times. We're from Seattle. I love it here! It's one of my favorite cities." I smile and look toward the driver, who smiles back at me in the mirror. Meeting new people makes me giddy, especially in New York. There is something genuine about them. They don't do fake. If they don't like you, you'll know it.

"How're you doing tonight?" I ask.

"Well, my day just got better." He's still smiling at me in the mirror. "New York is a great city. I've never been to Seattle. I hear it's beautiful and there's lots of rain."

"I've lived there all my life and it's still one of my favorite places. And yes, we get a lot of rain. That's what keeps it so green. How long have you lived in New York?"

"About ten years now."

"Wow. I'd love to live here someday." I feel warmly connected to this kind man, like I'm talking to an old friend.

The driver shifts his gaze to Derek in the rearview mirror.

"Is this your girl?" he says to Derek, who is staring out the window. "She's special, you know. She's a keeper."

"Yeah, I know." Wow, did Derek really agree?

"Do you love her?" Oh, my gosh, did he really just ask that? Derek's never said he loves me. He told me the first year we dated that he never would—that *you have to keep the girl guessing, 'cause as soon as you tell her you love her, she'll leave.* I hold my breath and wait.

"Yeah," he says apathetically. What? Did Derek just admit that he loves me ... to a stranger? I knew things were different, but this confirms it ... he loves me and he's going to ask me to marry him on this trip. I can hardly sit still. I can't believe it. It wasn't wishful thinking.

I lean against Derek's arm to let him know I love him too.

"Here is good," Derek says as the car slows to a stop in front of a busy restaurant.

"Okay. That's eight dollars."

Derek hands him some bills.

"Now you take good care of that girl. Don't let her get away."

I wait for Derek's response, but he's silent as we get out of the car.

We sprint down the street, passing several bars and restaurants before Derek stops at a door without any visible signage. Inside, there is a large wrap-around bar in the middle of the room and a dance song blaring. I hope we get to dance; that would be so much fun. I follow him to the bar. He hands me my drink and we climb some stairs to a loft area and find a seat on one of the couches near the dance floor.

The clear liquid in my glass smells like kerosene, but I taste it anyway. It's a vodka soda. I guess that's what I'm drinking tonight. Derek takes the last sip of his drink. Wow, he finished that fast.

"I'll be right back." He heads toward the stairs.

Derek returns with two glasses and hands me one of them. It's twice the size of my first drink and smells stronger. I gasp. It tastes like straight-up alcohol. I hold my breath and take a big gulp. It's gonna be a good night. Derek's always more fun when we're drinking.

Derek opens the door to our room and I stumble in behind him, nearly tripping over his suitcase. I still can't

29

believe he carried that garbage bag all over the city and ended up throwing it in the receptacle outside our hotel when we got back. Weirdo.

Wow, I drank a lot. Derek doesn't seem to be affected, but he does seem more relaxed. Thank God I don't have the spins. I think I feel a wave of alcohol traveling my veins. I feel good.

"Thanks for taking me out." He loves me. Why won't he say the words? It doesn't matter … I know he does.

Derek ignores me and walks over to the wall of shelves and retrieves something from a little box I didn't notice before. He joins me on the couch and puts what looks like a white powdery rock on the stainless-steel tabletop.

"This shit is pure," he says without taking his eyes off his little white treasure. "I only buy the purest rock, 'cuz I don't trust those assholes to not cut it with crap. You know what this cost? A thousand bucks. That's what you pay for the purest stuff. Only in New York. I've been getting it from the same guy here for years."

What? Is that cocaine? What's happening? Does he think I'm okay with this? I hope he doesn't expect me to do it with him.

He scrapes off some of the powder from the rock onto the table surface.

"You see how perfect this table is? You see why I stay at this hotel? It's the best. I only get the best."

I look up at the ceiling, searching desperately for something to transport me out of here. Is this really happening or am I having a drunken nightmare? I hear him

30

take a long sniff. I'm scared. What if he gets caught? Please don't ask me—

He stands and takes a couple steps to the desk and puts the little box back on the shelf. I look at the table and it's clean, no evidence in sight. He flops on the bed, grabs the remote, and navigates to something he must have liked earlier. Porn? Really? This must be a drug thing. At least he only does this in New York. I hope. He must've started this habit when he lived here for six years after his marriage ended. Maybe he'll quit if we get married. Ugh, highly unlikely and I can't marry a man who does drugs, even if he only does them once a year. Why can't he receive the love I have for him? He's insecure and acts out because he's been hurt, but I know in his own weird way he loves me. No one understands him like I do. I smile at him.

"Get that dopey look off your face and come to bed."

"You love me. I know it. Just say it."

"Whatever. Get your ass in this bed."

As I get close to the edge of the bed, he grabs my hand and pulls me toward him.

I take my place in the crook of his arm and snuggle closer to him as we drop off to sleep. Even though I wish things were different, these are the moments that make me forget all the reasons I hate this relationship.

Last Day in Paradise

This wasn't the trip I'd imagined. Instead of romance and sightseeing, we've scarcely left the hotel. And romance, well, I don't even know what that is anymore. Why did I think he was going to propose? I don't even want to marry him.

I fold my shirt and put it in my suitcase. We're supposed to leave the hotel in an hour and Derek is just lying there, staring at the ceiling. I'd say something, but he wouldn't hear me over the weird music he is streaming from his laptop. It sounds like something you would subject prisoners of war to ... and I feel like one. I shrug my shoulders to relieve some of the tightness.

Derek glances my way and turns down the music. "What the fuck is wrong with you?"

I'm exhausted. This week has been hell. You're an asshole, yes, I said it, ASSHOLE. Okay, I didn't say it, but the way you've behaved is deplorable. I feel sick. Sick of you and sick of myself for being here.

"Nothing."

"Then why do you look like a moron?" He's not gonna let this go.

"You're right, I'm an idiot. I thought you planned this whole trip for me and that you were going to propose. There, you happy now?"

"Have you lost your fucking mind? I'm never getting married again, not to you or anyone else. You really are a moron. As a matter of fact, I'm done. Find your own way home. I've spent enough on your dumb ass."

What? That's *it*? Two years of my life, jumping through hoops, trying to prove myself worthy of his love. Trying to get him to see that he doesn't have to be afraid of relationship … that I won't leave. I can't keep the tears from escaping my eyes. The sadness grips me like a beast that's finally awakened and I give in. I do my best to sob without making noise … until I can't.

"Oh, good God. Are you fucking kidding me. Get your sorry ass the hell out of my room."

I sob louder, zip my suitcase, grab my backpack and despondent, head toward the door. I look toward him and wait for him to say—*No, don't go.*

"What the fuck are you waiting for? Go." He waves his hand like he's sending away a dog.

I step out into the hallway and close the door.

What just happened? What do I do now?

The Abyss

I stare at the trees as each breeze introduces a dance of gold and rust colored leaves swaying soothingly, swirling around each other before finding their resting place on the grass. I have no idea how long I've been watching this mesmerizing autumn performance, or the details of how I got to this bench in Central Park. There is a numbness to the world around me as if I'm the woman-on-park-bench movie extra, meant to blend into the background.

I'm sure Derek is long gone by now. Maybe already home. I've never felt more alone, more unwanted. I still can't believe it happened. I can't believe he said those things. Did he ever love me? I've been replaying our relationship over and over in my head. What about the time he referred to me as his *significant other*? He actually said the words, *I have a significant other now*—like he was proud to be in a relationship with me. Or what about the time he surprised me for my birthday with a weekend trip to a beautiful bed-and-breakfast? He set up an entire day at a spa just for me, arranging all the details, including a massage, a facial, a manicure, a pedicure, a champagne lunch, and a haircut-and-style. Then he picked me up from the salon and took me for a long romantic drive through the country, ending the day with a gourmet dinner and a perfectly selected bottle of wine. What about our annual holiday drive through the neighborhoods to view all the twinkling lights? It was never something he enjoyed, but he enjoyed doing it for me.

Every tender memory causes a stabbing sensation in the middle of my chest. I feel like he ripped my heart out, flung it in a barrel, and each time I revisit those last moments together in the hotel room, he is stomping it to make his own blood-wine.

I don't feel like *being* anywhere. But I can't stay here all night. I search on my phone for *Hotels NYC*. Everything is either booked or a small fortune. Here's one for $89 a night, with a shared bathroom in Harlem. Part of me feels uneasy about staying in that part of the city. What if something happens to me? Part of me doesn't care.

I click on the *call* link, book a room for one night and make my way to my new temporary home.

I abandon my attempts to sleep and open my eyes to the beginnings of daylight streaming in through the slit between the faded orange-brown floral polyester curtains. A siren blares in the distance. After a fitful night's sleep, it's appropriate that I'd be awoken by an alarming sound.

I stare at the crack in the plaster ceiling, a flagrant metaphor for my life. I'm broken and I'm not sure I care anymore.

Wow. It's really over. I sob uncontrollably and am engulfed by the sickness in my stomach and the ache in my chest. Is this what it feels like to die? This can't be happening. My heart hurts. A deep, dull, inconsolable agony. I take a breath and pull the edge of the sheet to wipe away the disgusting slime of tears and snot that masks my face. Get it together, girl.

Why didn't my dad want me? Why didn't my sister love me? Why did my mom have to die? The preempted pain from every past tragedy in my life is consuming my attention. It's as if some invisible gate has been opened and I'm being trampled by a lifetime of accumulated grief. Another wave of anguish consumes me. Why did God take my son away? Why did *you* take him, God? I never did anything but love and try my best to do the right thing. And you took my mom and left me alone with a sister who hates me, then, as if that wasn't enough, you took my baby, my *son*—

You don't trust me interjects that familiar *knowing* in my thoughts. I've sometimes had this understanding in my mind that shows up and communicates with me, either imparting a revelatory truth or complete and utter nonsense. At some point, I decided to label it *God*, but it doesn't really matter what you call it. I could just as easily have called it, *It*, or *The Universe*, or *Higher Power*—but those words feel impersonal to me. So I chose "God." Author Elizabeth Gilbert once said, *all [these terms] are equally adequate and inadequate descriptions of the indescribable.* And I agree.

All I know is that when I pay attention to *it*, it brings me peace and things work out well. When I don't, I worry and things go poorly.

When people talk to God they call it *prayer*, but tell someone God talks to *you* and you're a crazy person. That's why I've never shared this part of my life with anyone, that is, until Dominic. He knew this about me the day we met in that small twenty-person church ten years ago. I don't normally go to church, but an old friend was so excited about their new church that I decided to check it out. After the service, Dominic introduced himself and when I shared my ideas about God, he told me I reminded him of a monk named Brother Lawrence. He then excused himself and returned with a copy of the book, "The Practice of the Presence of God." Brother Lawrence heard that voice or knowing in the same way I do and knew that there is nowhere we can go away from God—that he is present in night clubs, crack houses, prisons, board rooms, courtrooms, homes, everywhere. He worked for years in a monastery kitchen and believed that you don't have to go to the chapel to find God, that "you can find God just fine amongst the pots and pans."

I haven't trusted you, God, since my son died. Even though I thought I'd moved beyond this a long time ago, there it is. I never fully trusted you after that. Oh sure, I give you the unimportant stuff and pretend that you are a part of my life, but the stuff that really matters? I keep control of that, because *you can't be trusted with the important stuff.*

Wow, that's what I believe? I'm sorry. I don't want to feel this way. Help me feel different. Help me trust again. Help me trust you, God. I know you didn't take my son away, Sudden Infant Death Syndrome took him, but my heart doesn't know it. I don't know how to fix that. I don't know what to do anymore. I don't even trust myself.

I sit on the bed and glance around the room. It's not bad, just a little outdated.

"What now?" I say out loud, not expecting an answer.

Your best outcome is waiting for you. Let go and trust. The words flood my thoughts.

What? It's *waiting for me?*

You can take the long route and try to control everything, or the short route, and go with the flow of life, it's up to you.

I spend so much time in my head, strategizing how to get my way, how to manipulate the outcome which I *think* is best, yet that simple statement, "It's waiting for you," frees me from the suffering of forcing life to conform to my plan.

38

Take the step in front of you and trust that the next step will be there when it's needed.

Okay, God. I'll try.

✿

I've been lying here, crying, in my stark new reality for over an hour. This is pitiful. Maybe I can walk my pain away. I dress and head out onto the streets of Harlem. A short walk from the hotel, I see a sandwich-board for a coffee shop. I'm not hungry, but coffee sounds good. I descend the ten stairs to the door of the café, walk between the numerous occupied tables to the counter, order a drip coffee, and lean against a wall while I wait. I scan the room slowly. There are no computers or phones anywhere. Just people, seated together … talking to each other. My gaze lingers at each table, as I notice how engaged the people seem. No one is checking their phone … instead they are making eye contact, taking turns sharing. What a beautiful experience—to give and receive undivided attention.

"Drip coffee with cream for Anne."

"Thank you." I grab my coffee and walk toward the back of the café to an outdoor patio. I find an empty wrought iron table with two ornate chairs near a large mural with the word *Harlem* painted in white block letters on a turquoise background. I take a sip of my coffee and glance at the variety of people seated in the sunshine at the tables around me. There is one man, sitting alone, staring at a tree as if lost in deep thought. The others are engaged in conversation. Only one person with a computer and no phones in sight. Fascinating. A beautiful distraction from my painful thoughts. I reach into my backpack, retrieve my laptop, and refrain from checking my company emails. Focused on the scene around me, I attempt to capture the moment.

I finish the last of my coffee and look at what I've written. I've managed to portray a mood of connection … and an atmosphere of authenticity in my narrative of the outdoor café terrace with humans engaged in social interaction. I may suck at relationships, but I know how to paint a picture with words.

Screw him, he doesn't know what he's lost. He'll regret losing me someday. For a moment, I feel empowered. I gather my things and continue my walk.

My phone rings.
"Hey there, Dom." He really does have mysterious timing.
"What the heck? Why aren't you home yet?"
"I'm still in New York. Derek left already."
"Dammit. Why, did he leave you there alone?" I hear the frustration in his voice.
"Long story. But basically, we broke up and he took off without me … told me to *find my own way home.* I've stayed at a hotel the last two nights, and I think I'll stay a few more while I figure out what to do next. I feel so sad that I'm finding it hard to function—hard to think straight. I hate him and miss him at the same time. It's pathetic."

"Oh, Li'l Sprout, I'm so damn sorry, sweetie. It sucks that I'm not there to comfort you. You should get on the next plane and come home." His words reach through the phone and caress me.

"I'll come home soon." I reassure him. "I just need some time to deal with this. I can't stop crying and it's not just about the breakup, it's about every tragic thing that's ever happened to me. I never took the time to mourn the losses in my life. Every time something heartbreaking happened, I only grieved the amount that I couldn't control. As soon as I could get control of my sorrow, I've shut it down and moved on. And now I can't seem to control it at all."

"Here's a little secret for ya. It's supposed to hurt," Dominic says. "That's part of being human and how you know you loved. It sucks, but what if you're exactly where you need to be, emotionally? Maybe it's time to just feel and let go of trying to control it."

"It's weird you say that, 'cause the other day, I was thinking about trust and suddenly the thought occurred to me that I don't trust God, because I felt betrayed when my son died. And that's why I need to control everything, including my emotions, because—*no one* can be trusted." As I say the words, it feels like a puzzle piece clicking into place.

I need to let go of control. My heart's racing. This feels monumental, like I'm on the precipice of a change in my life.

"Holy shit, Anne, that's a big deal. I'm excited for you," Dominic says. "You know, you can't shut out the bad feelings without shutting out the good ones too. All of our emotions are essential to our well-being and the sooner we accept this fact, the sooner we become healthy and whole. You should watch the TED Talk by Brene Brown called *The Power of Vulnerability*. You can Google it. She talks all about this idea of controlling your emotions and why it harms you more than it helps."

Vulnerability, ugh. That sounds like more pain.

"Before you sigh at me," Dominic continues, "I know vulnerability sounds terrible and dangerous, like petting a bear with a steak. Believe me, I struggled with it. But embracing it is why we became friends and why I'm alive today."

I don't want to experience any more pain. For some reason, though, Dominic's words feel true.

"Okay, I will." Deep down, I know this is exactly what I need to do if I want to get beyond this.

"It's not for nothing, Annette." I hate it when he calls me that and he knows it. He only uses it when he's about to say something to piss me off.

"Don't call me Annette, ya jerk."

"Well, you should feel lighter now that Derek's gone, 'cause he only weighed you down every day that you were together," Dominic says. "He never treated you right and if you would've let me, I would've kicked his ass anytime. He was cruel, selfish, and an all-around shit sandwich. Sorry. Not sorry."

"I feel like I'm drowning. I don't know what to do."

"For starters, you need to begin taking care of yourself. Which means eating right and drinking less," he declares. "Also, get into motion, so the stress has somewhere to go. Instead of wallowing in your pain, breathe and go for a walk. And, not to get all religious on ya, but ask God to help you trust Him. He's there waiting for you to talk to Him. He has things to share with you, Anne."

Dominic has always been kinda in-tune with God. I've watched the surprised look of *how-did-you-know* on other people's faces when he tells them some private thing they're struggling with and that God wants to talk to them about it. He says that God tells him stuff and he passes it along.

"I've been telling myself, *the best outcome is waiting for you.*" I stop walking and lean against the wall of a building. "Remembering to surrender each day, is bringing me some peace. I've also been crying every day. There's a lot of pain in there, Dom."

"That's beautiful. You must purge the pain to make room for joy and peace." Dominic continues. "It's like pulling a splinter that's been festering; it hurts, but then the infection stops and healing can begin."

"I hope I'll allow myself to feel sad when it happens from now on, instead of holding it in."

"You will, because clearing the pain allows joy to take over."

"It's true. Happiness makes me cry now too, but in a good way. Who knew that all this allowing yourself to feel stuff could be a good thing?"

"I know. That's the strangest thing, letting those icky emotions work how they're supposed to, huh?"

Dominic says. "Everything beautiful comes from pressure and pain."

"Thanks, Dom, for being there for me."

"Of course. I've gotta go, but I'll be checking up on you. Hang in there, you got this."

✿

I open my eyes to the now familiar crack in the plaster ceiling. I can't believe I've been in this hole—physically and emotionally—for a week. I'm supposed to go back to work in a couple of days, but I need more time.

I've followed Dominic's advice and walked, cried and purged a lifetime of pain. I've had moments of debilitating agony and moments of surprising connection with people in the city. Dominic was right, when you allow yourself to feel the pain, you feel the joy more intensely. The time here has been good for me. I don't feel devastated anymore. The ache is still there, but it's no longer hijacking my attention.

I glance out the window at the building across the street. I'm not ready to face my old life. I have plenty of unused vacation and could extend my time away by a couple more weeks once I check in with my staff. But I don't want to keep staying in this dump.

My phone blinks. It's a message from my Facebook friend, James, who lives in New York. We've never met in person and I was supposed to contact him when I got to Manhattan. I found him online over a year ago, after reading his book on using music as a metaphor for selecting and enjoying wine, the philosophical stories he told about his life, sprinkled throughout the instructional information intrigued me.

I open my Facebook chat window. He's online.

Hi James!
[James] How's it going? Are you still in New York?
Yep, still here. It's been rough. This trip hasn't gone as planned. I may go home today if I can't figure out another place to stay for a while. Everything is booked, but if I work it out, let's schedule a time to get together. I'd still like to meet up with you.
[James] I'm sorry to hear that about your trip. I have an apartment in midtown that you could stay in for however long you need. I could have my cleaning person leave a key with the doorman for you. I know it may seem weird since we haven't met in person yet, and I completely understand if you feel uncomfortable.
That's very generous of you. But it is kinda weird. Let me think about it, okay?
[James] Sure. I was there last weekend and I won't be there again for a while. So, you would have the place to yourself.
Okay, I'll think about it. Thanks again, that's super kind of you.

Who does that? Who just offers up their apartment to a stranger? He's either a psycho or incredibly kind and trusting. At this point I'm not sure I care if he's crazy. I like the idea of having a week or two of not having to worry about what to do next.

James is still online.

Okay, I'm taking you up on your offer. I would love to stay at your place for a while. If it's not too short of notice, I could pick up the key today.
[James] That would be fine.
Thanks again. I really appreciate this.

The Trip Home

I gaze out the window of the 30th floor Manhattan studio apartment that I've had the privilege of staying in for almost two weeks. It's been nearly a month since one of the worst experiences of my life, and it's my favorite city again. I endeavor to capture in language the essence of the urban architecture—the historic buildings' rooftop menagerie with their big fan contraptions and random piping poking through tar surfaces, contrasted by contemporary buildings with their elegant patio gardens covered in elaborate seating areas designed to exploit the views. I've enjoyed the luxury of time to write. I want to continue this when I return home.

I still can't believe I'm here in this beautiful space. I'm grateful to James. It was all just so … divine … so perfectly perfect. A "God thing" that this apartment just happened to be available at the exact time I needed a place before I headed home. It's unbelievable that James let me stay here, free.

When we met for dinner last weekend, I unloaded my nightmare on him. He shared his own story of heartbreak and when we parted ways, I hugged him and said, "Thank you so much for everything."

He said, "You're welcome." And then asked, "Would you do me a favor?" He looked at me, his pleading eyes compelling me to say *yes* before I knew the question, but I waited.

"You know all that I've done for you while you've been here and how I've expected nothing in return?"

"Yes," I said.

"Well, when you get back to Seattle, I want you to remember that you deserve to be treated at least as well as I've treated you. Please promise me you won't settle for less."

I feel the moisture welling up in my eyes as I remember his words. He's right. In the two weeks that I've been here in his apartment, he's treated me like a princess and expected nothing in return. He's paid for everything and called and asked me every day how I'm feeling and had food delivered to the apartment for me. He even offered the use of his car, which of course I refused.

It's his compassion that's helped pamper me back to health. I feel the truth in his words, I deserve better, but is expecting better realistic? James seems like the exception, not the rule.

"I promise," I told him. I want my words to be true.

Even though it's been a rough few weeks, I've been miraculously taken care of the whole time. Just when I don't know what to do next, the next thing shows up along with the calm that comes with knowing it's the right thing.

My first thought every morning is still of *him*—nameless, he is now just initials in my phone—but at least now those thoughts run through my mind more like a movie reel, where you can think about a tragic scene without feeling the pain associated with it. I'm healing.

You're going to be fine ... better than fine, interrupts that familiar *knowing* in my head.

I realize it's true, I *am* going to be okay. *Thank you, God.*

☼

Gate B38. The screen behind the counter indicates my flight home boards in an hour. Home ... What does that even mean anymore? It'll be interesting to see if I fit into my old life, and if I don't, then what?

I've changed, but there is still an emptiness that pervades my life like an unnoticed homeless person trying to connect with passersby.

When I'm taking care of business, I feel powerful and in control. When I'm in a relationship with a man, I feel like a lost little girl.

It's time to stop trying to rescue men and save that lost little girl.

"Passenger, Anne Davis, to the ticket counter, please," says the woman's voice over the intercom.

"I'm Anne Davis." I hope nothing is wrong.

"Hello, Ms. Davis. We would like to offer you a free upgrade to first class today."

What? Wow. I glance at her name tag.

"Thank you, Anita. That would be awesome." I beam at her like a little kid who just won a trip to Disneyland.

"You're welcome," she says, and smiles gratifyingly as she hands me my new boarding pass.

This feels like a *sign*. Like, God is saying, *I'm offering you a first-class upgrade to your life. All you need to do is say, yes.*

Home - The Unsettling

I feel the downy comfort of my bed beneath me as I open my eyes. I look around my bedroom and notice all the carefully selected decorations. The two framed prints from my trip to Paris, my first time out of the country. The vase of roses that I dried to preserve the love I felt when Derek got them for my birthday, the first time he ever bought me flowers. The walk-in closet full of clothes, clothes that no longer *fit me*, accumulated over the last 10 years. Everything is familiar, but in an 'oh, I remember you' kind of way. I'm *home*, but this is no longer home.

Dominic's well-known ringtone blares from my phone on the nightstand. I must've forgotten to mute the ringer last night.

"Hi Dominic!" I don't want him to worry, so I do my best to sound happy.

"Morning, Li'l Sprout. How was your flight home?"

I feel my shoulders relax at the sound of his voice. I've missed him.

"It was great," I say. "I got a free first-class upgrade and I did some writing on the plane about my experience in New York. I feel better about the future, but I'm a little lost about what that future is."

"Oh no, Anne. Are you serious?"

"Wait, what did I say?"

"What you're experiencing is totally normal." Dominic laughs.

"Ya jerk. I'm glad you're entertained." I hate it when he messes with me like that. He gets great pleasure out of making me panic.

"Seriously though, you've been through a lot, and now you have some life-sorting to do. Can you meet me for coffee this morning?"

It'll be good to see him. Maybe he can help me figure out what's next.

"Sure. What time?"

"Meet me in about an hour at that little coffee shop by your house."

"Okay. See you soon."

"See ya."

I look for the end-call button on my phone and see that Derek is calling. Oh crap. Do I answer it? I trace the scar on my hand with my finger.

"Hello?" It's been several weeks since he kicked me out of the hotel room. What could he possibly have to say?

"Hi, Casper. Whatcha doin?" I used to love it when he called me that. Now I feel numb.

"Umm, not much. What're you doin'?" I wonder if he feels bad about the way he treated me in New York. Even if he does, I doubt he'll say anything. In the two years that I've known him he's never said he was sorry for anything.

"When do I get to see you?" His question lingers in the silence like an unclothed man who doesn't know he's naked.

"I don't want to see you." I can't believe those words came out of my mouth. Something has changed in me. "I don't want to be in a relationship with you anymore, and I'm not even sure we can be friends."

"Whaddaya mean? Come on, Casper, of course we can be friends. But if you don't want to, then I'm not gonna force ya." His nonchalance destabilizes me. I feel the familiar pull to make things right, but something bigger engulfs me and I'm grounded again.

"I just got home. I need some time to figure out what's possible with us before I can see you."

"Fine. Whatever. Call me when you *figure things out*." His sarcasm reminds me of how juvenile he can be and confirms I'm on the right track.

"Thank you for understanding." I feel empowered as I hang up the phone.

✿ DOMINIC

Ten Years Earlier

I feel the rumble of the V8 engine in my chest as I accelerate. The wind is pushing my hair back as it carries in the smell of the freshly fertilized field, a smell both offensive and familiar. Life couldn't get better. "You Shook Me All Night Long" is blaring on the stereo, and I'm heavy footed as I speed down the road. Freaking awesome! I can't believe I got this car, the only car I ever dreamed of owning, a '68 Mustang fastback with 380 thunderous horsepower propelling me into my future. Oh crap. I better get gas. I pull into the filling station and see a bright green banner with the words, "Do the Dew." I can taste the amazing lemon-lime goodness. Definitely need a cold one of those.

My eyes are pulled like they're attached to a string towards a woman walking into the filling station.
Nice ass echoes in my head.

As I reach the door, she glances my way with a *how're you doing* smile and my mind and emotions race to a place somewhere in the past. The static in my head tunes in to an occasional thought and my heart is pounding like someone kicking a garage door.

I feel dizzy. What the fuck?

I grab for the door handle with my sweaty palm and my hand slips off.

"Excuse me," I say and wipe my hand on my shorts without making eye contact. I reach for the door again, holding it open with my arm high enough for her to pass underneath. I tower over her small frame.

"Thank you, cutie," she says. She has bright blue eyes and light brown hair with small freckles around her nose. We make eye contact and she smiles flirtatiously. The small lines around her eyes tell me she's a bit older. But I'd certainly hit it.

Both aroused and repulsed, I'm confused by my sudden nausea.

She walks behind the register

"Hey, Janice, how are you?" says a voice behind me.

"That's it!" I blurt out unintentionally.

Everyone is staring. I'm the idiot yelling in an otherwise quiet store. I walk away from their stares and down one of the aisles.

I remember the last time I saw her, about sixteen years ago. She hasn't changed much. She's still hot. I feel like she has some mystic power over me. I can't stop looking at her. I better stop or I'm gonna creep her out.

I bump into a display. Slim Jims and bouncy balls scatter like they're fleeing my awkwardness. Once again, all eyes are on me. I scramble to pick up my mess.

"Hon, don't worry about it. I got it," Janice calls out from behind the register.

I ignore her and pick up the three items at my feet. She kneels next to me and picks up a bouncy ball lodged under some shelving. Her breasts are almost falling out of her not completely fastened shirt. Dammit, she caught me staring.

"Oops." She smiles playfully and secures the last button.

Get it together, Dominic.

I retrieve the last bouncy ball that escaped to the other side of the store and make my way to the Mountain Dew.

I've only been in this store for five minutes and I've made a complete ass of myself. Why am I so nervous around her?

Mountain Dew is on sale. Sweet.

"Have a goodnight, sweetheart. I'll see you tomorrow. Don't forget the cash drop," says another woman as she exits.

I scan the store. Janice is alone behind the counter and the store has cleared out.

I walk towards her and realize everything I think about saying doesn't sound right. I'm completely flustered by this tiny woman. I wiped out the store display and stared down her shirt. I guess there isn't much to say after that.

"Gosh, you look so familiar," she says as I approach the register.

"I'm Dominic. I don't think we've met before." Total bullshit. I know exactly where I know her from.

"I'm Janice. Do you live around here? Do you have a girlfriend? What do you do for a living?"

Oh, shit, she is hitting on me. I can't believe this.

"We should go out this weekend," she says.

"Yes, of course!" I say, way too loud and way too excitedly, grinning like an idiot.

I can't reconcile my feelings. I'm so excited and so full of anxiety at the same time. Is this just a case of the sexual tension between us or is it because she is older than I am.

"Can I have your number?" I stammer.

I take the number and head for the door.

"Dominic," she says as I reach the door, "did you still want these?" She holds up the twelve-pack of Mountain Dew.

"I swear I know you from somewhere," she says.

"We'll talk soon," I say.

I hustle for the door. I can't breathe, it's so hot in here.

Outside I struggle to connect with any thought other than *how could she not remember me?* After all we shared, something so intimate, something that I've always remembered.

My pager interrupts my thoughts. It's Josie. I can't wait to tell her that I saw Janice.

"Hello, Dominic!" Her bubbly voice shrieks from the phone.

"Geez, why are you yelling at me?"

"Oh, sorry. Hey, you need to come over. I need to talk to you about something."

"Okay, what do you want to talk about?"

"I can't tell you, just hurry up and get here."

"I can't. I'm supposed to go home and have sex with Danielle, the girl next door."

"You're a pig. You know there is more to life than sex."

"There is more, but nothing more fun," Dominic laughs.

"Ugh. Please come over. You can bang the neighbor anytime."

"Okay. I'll stop by for a minute. I have something to tell you, anyway. You won't believe it."

"Dammit, Dominic, you know suspense kills me. Like I almost literally die. What is it? You have to tell me now!"

"Okay. Do you know the gas station on Third Ave?"

"Yes. I go there all the time and I used to work there when I was in high school. I also used to date a guy from there."

"Hey, I thought *I* was going to share with *you*?"

"Oh, right. Go ahead."

"Well, I just stopped by and you won't believe it. They …" I pause for a few seconds.

"What? Tell me! I hate you for this."

"Okay, I went inside and guess what I saw?"

"Jesus, Dominic. What?"

"Geez, you need a Xanax. I saw that they have … Mountain Dew on sale."

"Dominic! You're an ass." she screams. I hang up the phone, basking in my own amusement. She hates being hung up on.

My pager goes off again. The familiar 3425 number, which on a telephone keypad spells out the word "dick." I chuckle as I open the car door and glance back towards the station's entrance, there she is, Janice, staring and waving at me. I wave as I start the car.

Journey's familiar song, "Faithfully" is on the radio. I sing along and with each verse a wave of emotion engulfs me.

Why am I crying?

I pull the car over to the side of the road. What the hell is happening to me?

I love Journey and enjoy belting it out, completely out of tune. Sometimes just to irritate anyone who has the misfortune of riding with me, while I sing obnoxiously. I've been collapsed by grief many times, but this is different. I have no idea why I'm sobbing. I can't stop.

I feel the tears stream down my face like a broken faucet. I can't breathe. My heart is going to pound out of my chest.

I smack myself in the head and kick the steering wheel's ass trying to get my composure back. It's nonsense to lose it like this and have zero idea why.

I rev up the engine, wipe the tears from my face and drive to Josie's house. I'm exhausted. I look in the mirror. I won't be able to hide these red eyes. What will I tell her? I take a deep breath and head for her door.

Josie

Josie races out the door and embraces me tightly, popping my back with her hug.

"Geez, creepy much?" I say.

"What do you mean?"

"Were you sitting in the window watching for me like a puppy?"

"Shut up and come in, you tool."

"Dominic, why are your eyes so red?" she asks.

"I was choking on something, that's all." I can't believe I lied to her, but I don't want to talk about why I was crying for no reason, while listening to stupid Journey.

"Are you getting sick?"

"No, Josie, just something in my throat, that's all."

Josie is one of the most caring and compassionate people I know. Her ability to love is why she's been a close friend for many years. I've told her my darkest secrets and she still loves me. She doesn't know that I have imagined her naked many times or that I fantasize about being her boyfriend. Those fantasies are usually snuffed out by her invasive personality, anyway.

"I need your help," Josie says. "Anne's upset with me."

"Why?"

"She broke off with another jerk and is already eyeing a new jerk. It sucks and I told her so. She is so much better than that."

"Josie, we both know that Anne doesn't want to hear from us anymore on this topic," I say. "Remember what she said, and I quote. *It's none of your business who I date.*"

"Yeah, but I can't stand seeing her throw herself into another horrible relationship. It breaks my heart."

"I feel the same, but she was clear and whether you like it or not we can't be a broken record. You have to stay out of it."

"Fine."

"We don't want her to avoid us again, right?"

"Okay, fine. You suck, but fine," Josie says. "So what did you want to tell me?"

"Well, for starters, I got my Mustang."

"No, you didn't."

"Yes. I most certainly did. I finally saved enough money and I can't believe the guy held it for me. I am so freaking happy."

"That's great, Dom. I'm happy for you," Josie wraps her arms around me.

"But, that's not the news I teased you about on the phone."

"Oh?"

"I noticed this chick when I was walking into the gas station and we shared a moment."

"I know about your moments, Dom." Josie says. "She probably had two real nice moments. We call them breasts."

"No, I didn't notice her breasts. I may have noticed her butt, though," I laugh. "No, this was something different. It felt as though I knew her my whole life. She's attractive but older and I couldn't place where I knew her from. All I knew is it felt weird. I was attracted and sickened at the same time. It took a couple minutes before I remembered how I knew her."

"You're a great storyteller, but would you please get to the point? Who the hell is she?"

"It was Janice. *Thee* Janice. Not only did I get the car I want today but I got her phone number and she asked me out. It's like I won the lottery."

Josie looks perplexed. I'm scared to ask her what's the matter. I stare at her and wait. I don't know if I've ever seen her so quiet and calm.

I nudge her. "Come on, wake up."

She takes my hand and looks me in the eyes.

"Dominic, you can't be serious. How could you possibly want to go on a date with her after what she did to you?"

"Well for starters, she didn't hurt me. She's hot and a bit older than me, which is even hotter. So why not?"

Josie looks at the ground.

I hum the *Jeopardy* soundtrack and smile.

She looks up at me. Tears stream down her face. I see so much pain and sadness. Her silence says nothing and everything. I've never seen her like this before.

I'm crushed.

"Please stop crying, Josie. You know I can't take crying. What's the matter with you? *Please stop. Please.*"

She sniffles and uses both hands to wipe the tears away that have made it to her cute little butt chin.

"I can't believe you're even thinking about dating her after all that she and her sister did to you," Josie says. "Like, it seriously makes me so sad that you'd even entertain the idea of dating her and even worse that you want to have sex with her. How could you? She is one of the most vile people on this planet. She damaged you and you show up all happy to tell me that you saw her? What did you expect? Did you think I'd be excited for you? Listen to me, Dom, you need to stay away from her. She's dangerous."

"Come on, Josie, she is as tiny as you. What could she possibly do to me? She is no more a danger than you are."

"Dominic, are you really that dumb? To this day, you're affected by what she did. It's controlled you your entire life."

"I'm fine, Josie. I'm on top of the world right now. Everything's going my way. She has zero effect on me. I'm one hundred percent fine. Absolutely, fine. What I shared with them was normal and special. You wouldn't understand, because you haven't experienced anything like what we had."

"What the hell are you talking about? You're wrong. You've never been fine. How can you not see it? You treat all women terribly. I think if I allowed you to, you would have used me and discarded me, too. You are incapable of having meaningful connections. You don't trust people and you keep them at arm's length. How is that fine?"

"Dammit, Josie, you don't know what you're talking about. You're freaking delusional. I can't believe you're attacking me. I came to share my great day and you shit all over it. It's none of your business anyway. You weren't there."

I storm to the door. She grabs my arm.

"Let go of my arm! You're ridiculous. I can't do this with you right now. I'm too emotional."

She looks startled as I pass her on my way out the door.

"Dominic, please come back. I love you. I didn't mean it."

I'm light-headed and nauseated as I stumble into my car. I don't recognize myself in the rearview mirror. This isn't who I am. What the hell happened to me today? I'm frustrated. Josie and I have had plenty of disagreements. Never have I walked out or been so angry at her. I glance back towards the house.

She's looking at me through the window. She looks so sad. What the hell is up with women staring at me through windows, anyway?

The tires squeal as I pull out of the driveway. I don't know where I'm going. I'm lost inside myself. I reach for my beeper that's going off. It's Josie's number followed by our code 423 meaning *call me now*, but I can't.

I drive and hope to settle the storm inside me. I'm exhausted. My eyes burn and I couldn't cry anymore if I wanted to.

Unearthed

I walk through my front door and am comforted by the familiar smells. It's the only place I want to be.

A memory of Janice and her sister talking to my mom in our living room commandeers my thoughts. I waited for them to finish talking and come in and get me to go play our game. We had hung out every day for a year. I waited day after day for them to come, but they never did. Why would my mom keep me from seeing them? I was devastated.

Silence and sadness follow me through the house, like a hungry cat bumping into me for attention. I sit down in my favorite chair and open a Mountain Dew and it's as amazing as ever.

There's a knock at the door.

Ugh. Please don't be Josie. I look through the peephole and see Danielle, the neighbor girl who comes over to "hang out" sometimes. She walks in, and gropes me as she walks by.

"Hey, cutie," Danielle says.

We have played this game for a few months now with no strings attached.

"How are you?" she asks.

"I'm having a tough day."

"I see you got the Mustang. Wanna take me for a ride and try out the back seat?"

She didn't even acknowledge that I'm having a bad day or that I clearly look like I'm in the dumps. Usually I'm excited to see her, but I'm not interested. Not even a little bit.

"Danielle, I can't right now. It's been a horrible day. Do you want to just hang out and talk?"

"You're joking, right? We don't talk, that's not the deal." She opens the door to leave. "If you change your mind you know where to find me."

Well, that's a first. This day has really been a piece of shit. I just turned away my sex buddy. Wow. I've never done that before. Janice and Josie are playing tennis with my thoughts and emotions. I can't do this alone. I need to talk to Anne. She's the only one I can trust right now. She knows me and will be honest with me. I clutch the phone and melt into my favorite chair.

"Good Tuesday morning!" blares my alarm. "It's 6:00 a.m., and as you make your way downtown, we have one accident to tell you about."

I wake up, slumped in my chair, still gripping the phone. That's right, I was going to call Anne. I rush clumsily

67

and hit my shoulder on the door jamb trying to shut off the alarm.

I need to make some sense out of this cloudy mess that's doing its best to collapse me under its weight. I dial Anne's number. With each ring the pit in my stomach gets deeper.

"Hello, this is Anne."

"Hey, Anne, it's Dominic."

"Hey, how are you? Josie just called me. She is worried about you and afraid you hate her now."

"Ugh. I could never hate her. Never. But she did piss me off and hurt my one feeling. You know how she can be. So pushy over something she knows nothing about. She wouldn't let it go."

"Well, I don't know what happened. She wouldn't tell me. She just told me that you guys had a disagreement and you stormed off, which you've never done before."

"Okay, so let me explain what happened yesterday. I bought my Mustang. You know, the one I've been saving for? I'm driving it around and I notice I need gas. So, I pull into a gas station to get gas and as I get out of my car, I notice a girl walking inside. Pretty damn hot. A little bit older than me, but well within the acceptable range. I head inside to pay for gas and we meet at the door. Something tells me that I know her from somewhere, just not sure where from—"

"Are you going tell me every detail or are you going to get to the point?" Anne interrupts.

"Okay. It was Janice. You remember, the Janice that I talked to you about. She didn't recognize me and she asked

68

me out. I was excited to tell Josie about this and she completely overreacted. Told me I should be disturbed by it."

"Geez, Dominic, Janice actually hit on you? Like she legitly wants to date you?"

"Yes, the feeling is mutual. I'm really attracted to her too. Although I felt a bit sick at the time. But it was probably just nerves because I hadn't seen her in so long. What do you think?"

"If I tell you, will you listen and not hang up on me?" Anne says.

"Of course, I promise. I'll listen. Scout's Honor."

"You're not a Scout, nor have you ever been one, ya jackass." This has been one of our stupid jokes for a long time. We get each other's humor. I'm grateful for her friendship.

"Come over. I don't want to do this over the phone." Anne says.

"Fine. Let me take a shower and then I'll be over. See you soon."

"Okay, butthead. Bye."

I grab my clothes and head into the bathroom, undressing as I walk. I check my pockets to get everything out. I pull out a receipt with her phone number. She signed her name and dotted the "i" with a heart. Damn, I was so distracted by Josie's reaction, I forgot to call her. I reach for my phone, wearing nothing but anxiety and my socks. Will she answer? Will she be upset that I didn't call yesterday? As it rings, a lump develops in my throat and my stomach starts to turn.

"Hello?" Janice says.

"Um, uh, hello," I stutter. "This is Dominic. You gave me your number yesterday."

"I know who you are. How are you? I waited for you to call yesterday. I thought maybe you weren't interested. I literally sat by the phone the whole night waiting and waiting."

"I'm so sorry. I don't blame you if you don't want to talk to me. I was so tired last night I fell asleep in a chair."

"I was joking. I'm glad you called."

"Oh, good. So how are you?"

"I'm really good. Except I thought about you all night. I just can't figure out where I know you from and it's driving me nuts."

"Maybe it's just that I'm the guy you've always dreamed about?"

"I don't think so." She laughs. "I know I've seen you before. Anyway, when are we going out?"

"Well, when are you free? I'm free anytime."

"How about now? You can pick me up and we can get something to eat. But I have to be back in two hours for work."

"I can handle that. What's your address?"

I take down the address and as I hang up the phone I remember that I was supposed to go to Anne's house. She'll have to understand. After all, I can't pass up this opportunity. I send Anne a page to let her know I'll be late.

I love the feeling of the wind blowing in my face. The cool air separates me from my thoughts as I drive to Janice's. A new song blares from the radio. It's that same damn Journey song I heard yesterday. I feel off balance. This is frustrating. I never let my emotions get the better of me. I've got to get this under control. It's messing with my life.

I shut off the radio. I can't stop thinking about Josie. Why haven't I heard from her?

I turn onto Janice's street and look for the house. My mind flashes images of a small boy riding up and down this street. I pass by a yellow '70s Ford Pinto parked on the street. I remember that car for some reason.

I feel like I'm in a bad home movie with poor clarity and zero dialogue. As I pull up to the house, I see an image of a little boy playing at the house next door. I remember playing on that porch. I lived there. The house numbers are still the same. As a boy, I had knocked one off and broke it, so my mom's boyfriend put up a mismatched one. I haven't been here in years. We lived there for two boyfriends, which is the same as two years. My mom changed guys about once a year as far as I could remember, each one more horrible and abusive than the last.

"Hey, are you going to sit there forever or are you going to come inside?" Janice is standing next to the car.

"Sorry. I had a long night. I'm *so* coming in." I wink.

"Are you okay? You look a little pale," Janice says.

"I'm fine. I didn't sleep well. I had an argument with my best friend yesterday, which has never happened before. But I'm good. Glad to be here."

"Oh, you poor thing," she says, leaning in for a hug that lasts way longer than it should've.

She takes my hand and walks towards her house. Her amazing scent is guiding the way. I take a seat on the couch

71

and she sits very close with her hand on my knee sending that tickle feeling up my spine and down my pants.

She is rubbing my leg.

"How long have you lived here?" I ask.

"I grew up in this house. My parents own it, but it's just me and my sister living here now. But she's not here. We are completely alone," she says, as she winks at me and slides her hand up my leg, where she finds out how happy I am to see her.

"Are you sure you want to get this started?" I don't know why, but I attempt to slow things down. Everything I did before yesterday was to get laid. Now I'm hesitating. What's my problem?

Janice can't keep her hands off me. She smells great and looks freaking fantastic. She marks off every box on the Dominic *I want to bang them* checklist. So why am I both turned on and repulsed?

Every breath I take feels like I am being strangled from the inside.

She moves in closer, puts my hand on her breast, and kisses me. My skin is hot and my mouth is watering like I am going to vomit.

I move her away from me and hop up. "Hey, I need something to drink. Do you have anything?"

"If I give you a drink, will you be a good boy?" Janice says. "There's Mountain Dew in the fridge, let me get you one."

I panic. "No, no, no. I got it!" I head quickly to the kitchen. I notice a picture stuck to the fridge of two teenage girls sitting on the porch of this house. They are hugging each other and giving the camera a thumbs-up.

My sexual arousal disappears quicker than my dad when mom mentioned child support. I remember the day they took this picture. I was standing next to their friend, the one who took it. They were giving the thumbs up to *me*.

I used to tell stories as a kid. Like the time I got this cool ass BB gun for Christmas or how my dad was able to come home for my birthday, but they were all bullshit. I'd watch movies then adapt the stories to my life, too ashamed of the truth. Like the fact that I hadn't seen my dad in years, but I told people he was in the special forces and away on secret missions.

I never had friends over and I learned that to make it in this world, you had to lie. I traded away terrible truth for glamorous lies. When you spend a lifetime lying, you become unable to tell the difference between your truth and your lies, so all memories are mixed up, blurry, or forgotten.

I glance at the picture on the fridge again.

I'm 5 years old, sitting in my living room, in the house next door. My mom comes through the front door with two teenage girls following behind her. She calls my brother Danny, then 9, in from the bedroom. There we stand in front of these two girls. My mom introduces them as Janice and Lisa. They are 16 years old and 18 years old. Mom informs us that they're going to be watching us at night while she is working. Which means we are free from

73

the abusive boyfriend she dumped once and for all after finding him with another woman.

The girls are fun. They let me stay up late, give me candy and lots of attention. I soak it in. About a month later, while my brother and I are watching TV, they give my brother candy and a Mountain Dew and tell him to stay put.

"Hey, where's mine?" I ask.

"It's in your room." Lisa says.

They follow me to my room and shut the door. I look around, but don't see any candy or soda.

"Where's the candy and Mountain Dew?" I ask.

Janice is holding a toy car, Mountain Dew, and candy. I lean towards her and reach for them.

"Wait. We have a deal for you," Janice says. "We'll give you lots of candy and soda, but you have to keep a secret and do what we say. You have to promise not to tell anyone. Not even your mom or your brother. It has to be our secret. If you tell anyone you won't get any candy or soda and we won't be able to watch you ever again. Your mom will have her new boyfriend watch you instead. Can you do that?"

"I can. I can keep a secret." I'm terrified of having another boyfriend abuse me. This was the longest amount of time where I hadn't been beaten daily. My body had healed and it felt good to be a carefree kid.

Lisa takes my hand and walks to the bed. She sits down and Janice stands behind me. I feel nervous.

"Can I have some candy now?"

"Relax. You're going to be fine." They giggle and Janice opens the soda while Lisa takes off her shirt. Janice hands me the soda and I take a big drink, then Janice removes her shirt.

"Put down the soda for a minute and come here," Lisa says.

I walk slowly to the bed where they are both sitting.

"Lay down," Janice says. "I'm going to help you change your clothes."

"But I don't want to go to bed right now. It's early."

"Silly boy, you're not going to bed yet. We are going to play a game."

I nervously lie down. They take off my clothes and their hands keep touching my privates but I'm not sure if this is an accident or not.

They remove the rest of their clothes. On hot days, I'd seen them in their bras, but never naked. I remember one hot day asking them when my chest would get big like theirs. "Hopefully never, sweetie," Lisa responded as the two of them laughed.

I notice they have hair where I don't and bruises all over their bodies. I haven't seen a woman naked before. I feel like I'm doing something wrong. They're smiling and talking to each other. I can hear their voices but not the words.

What's going to happen? Why are they doing this to me? I fidget. I'm sweating and my mouth is so dry I don't have spit to swallow.

"Can I have something to drink?" I ask.

"If I give you a drink, will you be a good boy?" Janice says, as she takes a sip of my soda, and then gives it to me.

I take a drink.

"That's enough," Lisa says and takes it from me.

They both climb into the bed with me and fondle and kiss my body. I feel uncomfortable, but I can't risk my mom not letting them watch me anymore. Even if I don't like it, at least it didn't leave bruises or make me bleed.

Beep, beep, beep!

Oh, shit. It's Anne. It's our code, 911, meaning urgent. I'm sure she's wondering where I am.

"Are you okay?" Janice is standing in the doorway to the kitchen.

Janice grabs my hand. Shivers race down my spine.

I yank my hand from her. "I'm sorry. My friend has an emergency and she needs me. I have to go."

"Right now? Are you serious?" Janice says. "You just got here. I thought we were going to have some fun."

She touches my crotch. I back up and forcefully push her hand away.

I run out the door.

"Call me later!" she yells as I head down the steps. I hop in the car and speed off, squealing the tires.

Innocence

Josie was right. I remember everything now.

As I reach for Anne's doorbell, she opens the door.

"What the hell is wrong with you?" Anne says. "We expected you a long time ago. We've been trying to get ahold of you and your ass doesn't respond."

"I'm so sorry. I was coming here … wait a minute, who the hell is *we*?" I step into the house and see a sad Josie walking toward me.

"Dominic, what's wrong? You look terrible!" Anne says.

"I'm a wreck. I just left Janice's house."

"Freak, Dom," Josie says. "Did you sleep with that girl? How could you? I told you she wasn't a good person."

"Why would you do that?" Anne says. "We know what she did to you. What were you thinking?"

They take turns yelling at me like cops conducting an interrogation, both speaking before the other has finished.

"Geez, calm down." I look at Anne and then at Josie. "I didn't sleep with her. I could've, but I didn't. She lives in the same house where she lived when I was 5 years old. So many memories came rushing back. It was like a movie reel that had been paused at age 5, started playing.

"I remember the feelings. It wasn't natural or special. It was horrible. What they did to me changed me forever. It's affected my whole life and all my relationships."

Josie rushes to me and hugs me tight. Anne joins in.

"What did I do to deserve that?" For the first time in my life, the memory of that experience feels dirty.

"No, Dom, you didn't do anything." Josie squeezes me tighter.

I have a sudden vision of a ball bouncing behind me and a young boy running to grab it. As I stare at him while he is smiling and his mom is yelling to look both ways, I realize that little boy lost something so precious. His innocence was taken away way too early.

I sob.

Anne and Josie embrace me and they are crying too. I've never felt so loved.

I'm heartbroken, but I feel like a great weight has been lifted off me.

We stay up until the sun comes up the next day. I pour out everything to them. I have never been this honest about my past with anyone, especially me.

I'm sad that I've mistreated so many women, but I'm thankful that Anne and Josie never fell victim to my sleazy ways.

Where do I go from here?

Like an inmate getting out of jail after many years, I'm awakened to the sounds of life and the hope of no more shackles.

I won't waste this moment, I promise myself. Somehow, I will make a difference and help walk others to freedom.

I sincerely hope you are one of them.

Today

Anne is like the sister I wish I had. She is so caring and self-sacrificing. Anytime I'm sick she is there to nurse me back to health. The problem is this desire to care for people has left her emotionally ruined, though most people would never know it. I never would've guessed that my nosy personality and a book would lead to Anne and me becoming the closest of friends. She was a small woman, standing behind huge walls that she'd built to keep people from getting too close. It was as though she was daring me to get close to her and I accepted the challenge. I could tell the second I met her that we had been down similar paths. We had an instant connection, one birthed in grief and pain. We both came to church looking for something to help us get beyond—or at the least decrease—the suffering we lived with every day.

Getting to know Josie and Anne were very different experiences. Josie was an open book. She was an aggressive friend, which meant she wouldn't let me *not* get to know her.

Anne on the other hand, was way more challenging. Whenever I learned something new about her, I would say "check," and she would punch me in the arm and tell me to shut up. Getting to know her took time. Every move had to be well thought out or I would risk losing her forever. I believe my willingness to take time is part of the reason we are friends today. Josie and I both are guilty of pushing too hard sometimes, even if out of love.

ANNE
&
DOMINIC

The Conversation

(Part One)

"Welcome home." Dominic wrapped his arms around Anne in a big bear hug and yelled, "Hey, lady, don't touch my ass!"

"Shut up. You're so embarrassing. I almost missed seeing your scruffy face." Anne playfully nudged his arm with her shoulder, stroked the five-o'clock shadow on his chin that he thought attracted the ladies, and took a seat across the table from him.

"What's that?" Dominic pointed to the small package that Anne placed on the table.

"Oh, my sister gave me one of those DNA tests for my birthday, and I'm mailing it in today," Anne said. "It kinda creeps me out to send my DNA to a company, but I figured, what the heck, it could be cool to find out my heritage."

"Interesting."

"Yeah, my mom was adopted and I never knew my dad, so who knows what I am." Anne laughed.

"You'll have to let me know what you find out. I've been curious about those tests."

"I will."

"How're ya doing?" he asked knowingly.

"I'm feeling better, but oddly that scares me. I'm worried that I'll go back to the way I was and nothing will change," Anne said, hurriedly. "By the way, Derek called right as I was hanging up with you. He wants to be friends and part of me still loves him and wants to help him, in spite of the way he treated me."

"First, take a breath. Second, you've gotta start with accepting today's happiness. Don't get ahead of yourself."

"That's the issue. I keep trying to determine the outcome instead of just focusing on the step in front of me."

"I know, you want a plan."

"Yep. Planner extraordinaire, that's me."

"Also, there's nothing wrong with caring for others," Dominic said. "You always will. That's just who you are. But the most important thing you can do is care for yourself *first*."

"You're right. I go out of my way to take care of everyone but me," Anne said. "Also, I ignore the truth about the relationship to stay in the relationship. I construct the story I want to believe and seek evidence to back up my false belief."

"Spot on. And that makes you a normal human."

"How do I stop doing that?"

"That's what people do when they can't accept the painful truth of their reality."

"If I'm being honest, part of me still wants the relationship with Derek and hasn't completely let it go. But it makes me feel weak to admit it."

"You've driven on Seattle's pothole-ridden roads, right?" Dominic said. "How do they fix them?"

"Fill them?"

"Fill and repave. They can never go back to what they were, but they can be covered and made new, thus eliminating the old holes of problems, pain and regret."

"I get it. That's where I always get stuck, clinging desperately to the hope of going back to when the relationship was good."

"And in doing so, you never give relationships the opportunity to be new and better. You cheat them out of their potential."

"You're right!" Anne said, excitedly. "I decide that the relationship must either go back to the way it was or it has to end."

"It's the same as if you decided to put on a diaper and try and pretend you're a baby," Dominic said. "You know damn well you're not, but that's the point where you know there wasn't pain. You want to go back in all relationships to the point where there wasn't any pain and when you can't, you throw them away. Because you can't risk being in pain."

"Bingo. That's totally it." Anne stared off into the distance.

"Yes, it is," Dominic said, matter-of-factly. "The fix is in the future, the reason is in the past." Dominic is purposely cryptic to both entertain himself as well as to persuade Anne to think.

"The fix is to build something new?" Anne ignored the smirk on Dominic's face and attempted to understand.

"Yes. You must be honest with yourself about the relationship today and decide how to move forward from here. Then, do it. You *repave.*"

"Ah, got it."

"This is how you breathe life into all relationships from this day forward. Thus, taking them into truth."

"I like that ... *breathe life,* taking them *into truth,*" Anne said.

"It's not about *eliminating* the past, but about taking away its power over us," Dominic said. "Sometimes a seemingly unworkable relationship doesn't have to end. Instead, it can be transformed into something new."

"This morning, I read through a bunch of journal entries from almost ten years ago, at the end of another relationship, and you could literally switch out the guy's name for Derek's name and you wouldn't know the difference—the shock that he didn't want to be with me, the struggle to let go of the relationship, the desperation to stay connected in any way he would allow, et cetera. All the same, just a different name. It's crazy and depressing."

"We live in cycles," Dominic said.

"But I don't want to live in that cycle!"

"You aren't. That's the old you."

"God, I hope so," Anne said.

"So, from this point forward, in any situation, you need to ask yourself, 'What's the benefit? If there's no benefit, don't do it. Otherwise, it'll lead to pain."

"Okay. That makes sense," Anne said. "The most significant thing I've learned so far is to stop running from pain. I've had many losses in my life that I've never allowed myself to fully *feel*. The death of my son was a big one. All that pain preempted by a need to *be strong*. By allowing myself to *feel* the pain, I've opened my heart to the joy."

"All emotions have their purpose and importance," Dominic said.

"I've always cared about people, but now instead of ignoring the person talking to themselves on the subway, I make eye contact and acknowledge them with a smile. You know, when he got off the train, he mumbled under his breath, *thank you for noticing me*. I cried. I feel forever changed by this time in my life. I feel like a kinder, gentler version of myself."

"I'm extremely proud of you," Dominic said. "You've come a long way in a short time. It shows your resolve and desire for the future to be beautiful. You aren't alone and people love you."

"I'm starting to figure that out," Anne beamed.

"You just had to surrender control."

"I'm learning to be okay with the unknown," Anne said.

"Walking in the dark room before you turn on the light."

"Good analogy."

"Thanks, I'm full of them."

"You're full of something." Anne winked.

"The goal is to keep taking steps forward. Keep purging your life of that which isn't beneficial."

The Conversation

(Part Two - One Month Later)

"Hey, how are ya?" Dominic stood up from the booth in the café where they met a month earlier and hugged Anne in an unhurried way, like he knew she needed it.

"Sad." Anne slid into the booth across from him. "The holidays are rough. Been crying most of the day."

He nodded in understanding. "Is it because of being alone?"

"Yes. I'm exhausted. I'm done being the pillar of strength for everyone."

"That's good, 'cause you can't be anymore."

"I can't and don't want to."

"Good," Dominic said approvingly. "You have any plans for the holidays?"

"Yeah. Going to a party tonight. A candle-lighting service tomorrow. Staying busy."

"That's good. Let the pain out. Stay busy, but let the pain out."

Anne took a sip of her extra hot mocha, which was now lukewarm.

"You'll get past the pain, I promise," Dominic smiled.

"Okay," Anne said. *I want to believe him. No, I **need** to believe him.*

"It's good to let the pain out, but don't stay there."

Anne glanced out the window and wondered what was next for her. For the first time in her life, she felt closer than ever to breaking free from her pattern of tolerating bad relationships. But she wondered, *is that true, or just wishful thinking? How do I know if anything has changed or if I'm still the same idiot who's been told her picker is broken—?*

"Hey, Josie, over here!" Dominic waved to an attractive, petite woman with long, dark, wavy hair, who was standing near the door to the café. As she approached the table, Anne recognized her.

"You remember Josie?" Dominic asked.

"Of course I do." Anne smiled and wrapped her arms around Josie, whom she hadn't seen in over a year. "It's good to see you again."

"Good to see you, too, Anne." Josie smiled as she slid across the bench next to Dominic.

"I asked Josie to join us, 'cause I thought she could offer a different perspective. She's a *feeler*," Dominic said.

"Yep. Which frustrates the hell out of Dominic, cause he's a *doer*." Josie laughed playfully. "He hates us *feelers* with all our pesky little feelings."

"What are you guys talking about?" Anne asked, as she looked at Dominic for the answer.

"Oh, I guess we've never talked about that, have we?" Dominic said. "Well, I've found there are three types of people. Doers, feelers and thinkers. Doers, like myself, are goal oriented. They don't have time for emotions. Feelers are driven by emotions. All decisions are based on feelings. Thinkers are driven by logic. Everything is a thought process. Their decisions are disconnected from feelings."

"I'm a *thinker*, aren't I?" Anne said. *That explains why I overanalyze everything.*

"Yep," Dominic said. "That's why it's important for you to feel. To get out of your head."

"And that's why Dom thought I could help, 'cause I'm all about feelings." Josie winked at Dominic.

"Well, yes, that and the fact that you have a way of helping people see things they'd never see on their own, especially those who aren't feelers." Dominic mischievously grinned at Josie.

Anne suspected there was a story there, but decided to leave it alone. "I'm happy you're here, Josie. I welcome all the help I can get."

"Aw, thanks, Anne." Josie smiled, then reached into her bag and pulled out a pad of paper and a pen, and pushed them across the table. "So, I thought we could start with an exercise I did several years ago that really helped me. I think this is a good way to connect with some of your feelings about important events in your life and you don't have to share what you write, unless you want to."

"Okay," Anne said, tentatively.

"It's fairly simple. You make three columns, with the headings, *age, event,* and *feelings.* Like this ..." Josie reached across the table and drew on the paper in front of Anne. "Then you list every significant event in your life, from birth until now. Write your age, what the event was, and a couple words that describe what you felt about that event, like happy, sad, etc. And by *significant,* I mean, significant to *you.*"

"When Josie told me about this, I knew it was something that could help you. Whaddya think? Wanna try it?" Dominic asked.

Anne glanced at the chart in front of her. "Sure, I'll give it a try." *I don't know how this is supposed to help, but I trust Dominic.*

"We're gonna go grab a bite to eat. We'll be back in a bit," Dominic said.

"Okay. Wish me luck," Anne said.

"You don't need luck. It'll be good. You'll see." Dominic grinned, as he escorted Josie to the café exit.

An hour later, Anne put down the pen and stared at the sheet of paper. Front and back, two-pages that represented every significant event in her life.

The first column, *Age* ... zero. The second column, *Event* ... Born. The third column, *Feeling* ... Don't know. She scanned the page.

Age four. Mom gets breast cancer. Scared.
Age six … Sad.
Age eight … Scared and alone.
Age ten … Sad and scared.
Age eleven … Sad and alone.

Age twelve—*oh my god.*
  Mom gets bone cancer. Sad and scared.
  Sex for the first time. Sad and alone.
  Pastor shut me down spiritually. Sad and alone.

Wow. Those things all happened the same year. Age twelve, the most impressionable time in a life.

Tears streamed down Anne's cheeks.
Her eyes lingered on the middle line …

Age twelve. Sex for the first time. Sad and alone.

I've always worn my youthful sexuality like a badge of honor. Proud to say, I had sex younger than most, like that makes me sophisticated—

Dominic approached the table. "Josie had to run an errand, so she'll be back in a little bit. How's it going?"

"This is unbelievable," Anne said. "You remember when I told you I had sex when I was twelve and it freaked you out? And I couldn't understand why you got so upset and wanted to put the guy in jail? I get it now."

Anne's gaze lingered on the three lines reading *age twelve.*

"I was raped."

She looked at Dominic and waited for him to say something, but he was not shocked. He already understood what she was just now realizing.

"I was only twelve years old! I was in no position to make a choice like that. I had no idea what I was getting myself into. The adults around me should've protected me. What the hell?"

"I know," Dominic wrapped his arms around Anne, and she sobbed into his chest.

ANNE

Twelve Years Old

Anne meandered down a large corridor on her way to her next class. She loved the high ceilings, big arched windows, and ornate molding of the historic, two-story brick building. It was captivating compared to the one-story, institutional-looking elementary school she'd come from, but she didn't care much for the student culture that came with her new junior high school. At her old school, she could talk to anyone she thought was interesting. Here, there seemed to be some kind of protocol involving your appearance that determined if you were allowed to make friends.

Anne's mom had moved them to Ballard three months earlier because she read an article about young girls being kidnapped and turned to prostitution in their urban neighborhood and was worried about Anne entering puberty amongst the expanding "criminal element."

Anne, tardy for her 4th period French class, approached the wide staircase, which looked like it belonged on the ship, *Titanic*. She heard voices coming from the top of the stairs. She glanced up and saw three tall, thin, Scandinavian-looking boys shoving a shorter dark-skinned boy.

"Where's the flood, boy?" said one of the blonde guys as he kicked the shorter boy just below the knee, setting him off balance and down the stairs. The hemline of the boy's jeans, which were about two inches above his shoes, revealed his white socks; an unintentional style known as high-waters.

His tumble landed him about halfway down the staircase, where he sluggishly stood and hobbled the rest of the way to the bottom of the stairs, about three feet away from Anne.

"Leave me alone." His demand did nothing to deter the other boys, as he wiped the blood from his nose with his sleeve.

"Leave me alone." The tallest guy, who seemed to be the leader, mocked him in a high-pitched voice as he made his way down the stairs with the other guys following behind him. "You gonna go cry to your mommy?"

The boy tried to navigate around them, but was blocked as one of them stood in front of him, another knocked his glasses off his face, and another shoved him. The boy stumbled backwards and with a sweeping gesture, saved his glasses before they hit the floor.

"What're you doing here anyway? You don't belong here. You should be with your kind."

Anne stood motionless as tears streamed down her face. She sensed the boy's physical pain and emotional trauma as distress in her body; she felt his panic in her throat, his aching for acceptance in her chest and his humiliation in her abdomen. From the time she was six years old, she could feel the suffering of others as if it were happening to her.

The leader shoved the boy again. "You gonna answer me, boy?"

"Leave. Him. Alone." Anne was energized by the force of the words that came from somewhere deep within her. She felt no concern for her safety, as she knew that she was acting in cooperation with a strength greater than herself.

The tall blond turned toward Anne.

"Oh, look what we've got here guys, we've got a nigger lover."

Anne was in shock. *Is this really happening? Did he really just say that?* She was devastated when she learned about slavery and prejudice in history last year. She couldn't comprehend how anyone could inflict such cruelty on another person simply because of their skin color. She attended school with kids from diverse cultures, economic status, as well as varied physical and mental abilities. Some of her friends lived in mansions and some in tiny apartments like herself; Some had two moms or two dads and some had crooked bodies that got around on crutches; Some could only make noises in their attempts to form words and some needed the school staff to spoon feed them at lunchtime. Anne noticed their differences, but not in the way that makes someone decide a person is good or bad. She saw their differences as something which made them more interesting. She couldn't believe that there was a time when people saw a difference such as race as something that made a person bad and was relieved to believe that times were different now. But she had no idea there were those who still thought and acted that way.

"Hey, I'm talking to you. Did you hear me?" said their leader.

"I said, *let him go*," Anne firmly responded.

"Whatcha gonna do about—"

"What's going on here?" interrupted the booming voice of Anne's homeroom teacher.

"Nothing, Mr. Adamsen. We were just heading to class." The leader of the pack waved his hand for his buddies to follow and they disappeared down the hall.

Mr. Adamsen turned toward the battered boy and glared. The boy seemed to hear the silent command, "Go!" and hustled down the hall in the opposite direction from the other guys.

"Get to class, Miss Davis." Mr. Adamsen focused on Anne as he waited for her to comply.

She hesitated for a moment. *Why didn't he do anything? He obviously knew them. Had they done this before?*

"Now. Miss Davis." The force of his voice startled her and she stumbled over the first step before making her way up the stairs.

She opened the door to the one-bedroom apartment where she lived with her mom. It was bigger than the one-room studio they had come from in the city. She was happy to have her own bedroom even though her mom still had a bed in the living room.

"Mom!" Anne called out.

"In here." Her mom's voice echoed from the kitchen.

Anne anxiously peeked around the corner and saw her mom sitting at the table.

"Where's Julie?" She'd only seen her big sister twice; once when Anne was 6 years old, then about three years ago around Christmas. Julie's dad had taken her from their mom and she ran away at age 16, as soon as she was able to support herself.

"She should be here any time now."

Anne had been looking forward to this visit for weeks; she hoped she could convince her 21-year-old sister to live closer so they could spend more time together.

Anne ran to answer the knock at the door.

"Where's mom?" Julie said.

"In the kitchen." Anne's beaming smile faded as she stepped aside and let Julie into the apartment. Anne followed her sister.

"Anne, I need you to go to your room for a little while ... I need to talk to your sister alone." She hadn't seen her mom look that serious since the time when she was 8 years old and her mom told her that their neighbor and close friend had died.

Anne trudged to her bedroom and closed the door. She sat on the bed and brushed the fur of her stuffed tiger with her fingers while staring at the closet. Outside her door she heard the muffled voices of her mom and sister. The fear crept through her body as she listened to the sounds coming from the living room escalate from quiet murmuring to hushed whimpering. She reached for the library book, *Love and Living* by

Thomas Merton, from the stack of books she was currently reading. It was not a typical book a middle-school student would choose to read, but like her mom said, she was precocious even as a child. Her mom liked to tell the story of 3-year-old Anne who, upon witnessing her 2-year-old cousin throwing a temper tantrum, looked up at her mom and said, "That's disgusting." They say the apple doesn't fall from the tree, so it was no surprise that her mom was a walking encyclopedia with a vocabulary that would make an English professor jealous.

She opened to the bookmarked page and read:

> *But the question of love is one that cannot be evaded. Whether or not you claim to be interested in it, from the moment you are alive you are bound to be concerned with love, because love is not just something that happens to you: it is a certain special way of living and being alive.*

Anne grew excited as she often did when she read something she already had a deep knowing about.

She knew that love was the force that permeated and connected everything. When people spoke of intuition or spoke of God, she knew they were talking about love—the essence of truth that never changed. The truth that was embedded in every person like a built-in guidance system providing an innate sense of right and wrong—not the right and wrong that adults seem to use to judge each other, but the right and wrong that stemmed from the simple question of "Is love in it?" ... If it was, it was right. If it wasn't, it was wrong.

She hoped she would never lose this awareness of truth and become like the adults she knew. They were afraid of themselves and afraid of each other. They couldn't see themselves clearly and not only judged others, but judged themselves even more harshly. Many of them allowed themselves to be abused because they didn't know how beautiful and valuable they were. And some of them hurt others because they were hurting so bad they thought they could lessen their own pain by inflicting it on another.

Anne understood that the only answer to any question was love ... when you extended love to another or to yourself, you were wholly in line with your guidance system ... everything else was just details. She thought about the boy at school and wondered if he was okay. She wished she could've reached out and hugged him and told him everything was going to be okay, and not to listen to those other boys.

Her thoughts returned to the conversation outside her room which seemed to have fallen silent. She peeked out her door and saw them seated in the living room.

"It's not fair," Julie said.

"I know, but there's nothing we can do about it."

Her mom turned toward Anne in the doorway.

"Come in, sweetie. We're all done."

Anne walked tentatively toward the living room.

"So, how was school today?" Julie asked.

Anne knew something was wrong, but didn't understand why they were pretending everything was okay. She reflected on the incident at school and her confusion transformed to sorrow. She wanted to tell her mom about it, but the distant look in her mom's eyes held her back.

"It was fine," Anne answered.

Anne helped her mom clear the dirty dinner bowls from the small kitchen table. She hated lima bean soup—the mealy texture and the bland flavor disguised with salt—but that seemed unimportant, given the bizarre way her mom and sister were acting, so she'd eaten it without complaint.

"Hey, Anne, wanna go for a walk?" Julie said.

"Sure." Anne hoped if they left the apartment her sister would perk up. She slipped on her rain jacket, sprinted to the door and waited.

"Come on, Julie." Anne was excited to spend some time alone with her big sister.

"I'm coming."

They made their way down the two flights of stairs and out onto the glistening sidewalk. It had rained

earlier and the air smelled like damp dirt and cement—
the only fragrance Anne loved more was freshly mowed
lawn. She skipped a couple of steps and glanced up at
Julie. The voluptuous shape of Julie's lips and her
delicate turned-up nose reminded Anne of Stevie
Nicks. She wished she were as pretty as her sister—so
feminine, so sultry—the kind of beauty found on
posters adorning the walls of teenage boy's rooms.

"I have something serious to tell you." Julie's
words startled Anne out of her dreamy-eyed gaze. She
stared anxiously at her sister's face and waited.

"Anne, mom has cancer. The doctor said she
only has three months left to live," Julie announced, not
looking at her little sister as they continued down the
street.

Anne frantically watched her big sister for a sign
that this was a cruel joke or maybe she heard her wrong,
maybe she was talking about someone else's mom, or
… something else, anything else.

"I don't believe you." Anne's statement begged
her sister to say it wasn't true.

"I'm sorry, sweetie. Mom got a call from the
doctor earlier today with the results. I wish this wasn't
happening. It's not fair. Mom asked me to take care of
you when she's gone."

Anne lumbered forward in silence. Under any
other circumstance, she would've loved the idea of

living with her sister. But she didn't want to be without her mom. And why was her sister acting so matter of fact? She didn't even seem sad. Anne had overheard Julie once ask their mom why she hadn't fought for custody, but whatever reason their mom gave her, it didn't satisfy Julie. Sometimes Anne felt like Julie resented her for being born, for having the relationship with their mom that Julie wanted. But Anne was convinced that she could win her over. Once Julie got to know her, she would love her and be happy to have her as a little sister.

And if their mom died, she'd have to love her ... wouldn't she?

She barely kept pace with her sister as her eyes welled up and sadness flooded her tiny body.

✿

Anne watched two of Julie's big guy friends carry the last two boxes from their truck into the house. The doctors had been wrong, after all, but not in the way she'd hoped. Her mom was hospitalized two weeks after she was diagnosed and died one week later. Julie's church had held the funeral last week, but her pastor had talked more about Jesus than their mom.

"That's it," one of the guys said as he grabbed a beer from the six-pack his buddy was holding. "We're gonna take off. Thanks for the beer." He nodded the bottle in Julie's direction.

"Thanks, guys. I couldn't have done it without you." Julie walked over to him and kissed him on the cheek.

He patted Julie on the butt. "No problem. Anytime, baby." And he strode out the door with his friend following close behind him.

Julie walked over to the pile of boxes and examined them to decide which to unpack first. She'd been the one responsible for dealing with the estate. Anne thought it was strange to call the thrift-store contents of a two-bedroom apartment an estate, but that's the word that the legal guy used. She'd had no say in what was kept and what was left behind. So, all that made it to the 700-square-foot, two-bedroom rental house where Julie lived were three small boxes filled with kitchen stuff and knickknacks, a rocking chair and a medium-size box of Anne's clothes and toys. Since Julie had not chosen to keep any of their mom's books, Anne slipped one of them, *The Aquarian Gospel of Jesus the Christ,* into her medium-sized box when Julie wasn't looking. Their mom loved to read and did so constantly—magazines, newspapers, books—and Anne longed to stay connected to her through written words.

Anne trod through the kitchen and hiked the narrow staircase to the attic area that served as the second bedroom in the house. There was an alcove with a sheet hanging from a curtain rod, which functioned as the closet, and a tiny square window at the peak of the angled ceiling which allowed in daylight. The only furniture was a twin mattress on the floor. She dragged her box of stuff over to the bed and began to remove items: her clothes, the shiny black case of Barbie dolls and their clothes, the swimming pool her mom made for her dolls out of Styrofoam, her copy of the book, *The Phantom Tollbooth* (which she received as a gift when she was 9 years old and was engrossed in its Kingdom of Wisdom for twelve hours straight until she reached the last page), and lastly, the book that had belonged to her mom. She leaned back on her pillow and opened the book to Chapter One.

✪

"Anne! You need to get ready for church!" Julie hollered from downstairs.

Anne rubbed her eyes and rolled over. She had stayed up late reading and wasn't ready to wake up.

"I'm awake," she yelled back.

"We're leaving in 20 minutes."

"Okay."

Anne threw off the covers and pushed herself up from the bed. She changed out of her pajamas and into a long-sleeved, navy blue sweater and jeans, which were the best pieces of clothing she owned. She wanted to look nice for her sister and was excited to be with others who experienced knowing like she did, people who knew God. In the six months since their mom died, Anne had done her best to help her sister and not be a burden, but there were times when she felt Julie didn't like her. Like the time she overheard Julie tell someone that their mom had spoiled Anne and that's why Anne was a know-it-all.

She reached the bottom of the stairs. Julie was seated at the kitchen table drinking coffee and glanced toward Anne.

"Good morning, sleepy head. There's cereal if you're hungry."

"Good morning. Cereal sounds good, thanks." Anne poured milk into her bowl of Raisin Bran that Julie had put out for her, and took a seat at the table across from her sister.

"How'd ya sleep?"

"Okay, but was up kinda late reading a book."

"Oh yeah? Whatcha reading?"

"Um … I can't remember the name of it. Just some story about a man who lived a long time ago." Anne was afraid she'd get in trouble for keeping their mom's book.

"Oh, by the way, I'm having a party next month and Marvin is coming up from California with some friends." Julie took a sip of her coffee.

"He's coming all the way from California for the party?" Anne realized as soon as the words left her mouth that their step-brother was probably coming to town for the holidays.

"No, he's visiting his grandma and cousins for Christmas." Julie got up from the table and put her mug in the sink. "You ready to go?"

Anne took her bowl to the sink. "Yes, I'm ready!" She hoped her enthusiasm would make her sister forget her stupid question.

"Well, good morning, ladies." Pastor John smiled at Anne and her sister.

"Good morning, Pastor." Julie reached for a program from the stack next to the entry and found a seat toward the back of the room. Anne slid next to her on the pew and noticed the words "Do You Want to Burn in Hell?" at the top of the church handout Julie was holding.

A woman who looked like she stepped out of an episode of the TV show, "Leave it to Beaver," walked across the stage and took a seat at the organ. Everyone became silent as she played a song that reminded Anne of a funeral she'd seen on one of her mom's favorite soap operas, *The Young and the Restless.*

The pastor walked by their row on his way to the stage.

"Good morning, everyone. Today's sermon is about the beautiful blood of Jesus and how to make sure you're saved from the wrath of God and from burning in hell for all of eternity. We know we're all sinners, but do you know for sure you're saved and are going to

Heaven? This is what we'll talk about today, and at the end of service if you're unsure about your salvation, you'll have an opportunity to get saved today. But first let's honor our Savior with a song."

Julie handed the red book to Anne, who opened it to the page with the hymn titled, "Heaven and Hell." The woman at the organ led the singing:

> *There is beyond the sky*
> *A heaven of joy and love;*
> *And holy children, when they die,*
> *Go to that world above.*
> *There is a dreadful hell,*
> *And everlasting pains:*
> *There sinners must with devils dwell*
> *In darkness, fire, and chains.*

Anne shifted in her seat. *Did we really just sing about dwelling with the devil in darkness, fire, and chains? Why would there be chains in hell? That's ridiculous.*

The singing continued.

> *Can such a wretch as I*
> *Escape this cursed end?*
> *And may I hope, whene'er I die,*
> *I shall to heaven ascend?*
> *Then will I read and pray,*

While I have life and breath,
Lest I should be cut off today,
And sent t' eternal death.

Anne examined her sister to see if she was upset by those words. *Does she believe this stuff? She's a wretch?* She watched Julie sing the last verse along with everyone else, with no sign that she disagreed.

The pastor spent the next thirty minutes describing the place called Hell where people who don't accept Jesus Christ as their lord and savior, otherwise known as sinners, are going to burn for all of eternity. When he finished his speech, he asked for volunteers to come forward and get saved to guarantee their place in Heaven.

Julie whispered to Anne. "Do you want to be saved? I can go up there with you?"

Anne didn't believe anything she'd heard in the last half-hour, but she didn't want to disappoint her sister.

"Um … sure."

✧

Anne flopped on her bed and thumbed through the pages of the Bible that Pastor John had given her after the service. In the back of the book there was a glossary of words and their meanings. Her thoughts wandered back to the sermon. *What is sin?* She found the word and read the definition: *Miss the mark. So, a sinner is someone who missed the mark? Wow, that's it? I think Pastor John missed the mark with his sermon, he must be a sinner.* Anne giggled at the thought.

The more she read, the more excited she became as she recognized aspects of the God of her understanding within its pages. *I want to be a pastor. I want to share the truth about who God really is and help people instead of make them feel bad about themselves.* She leapt off the bed and sprinted down the stairs.

"Julie!"

"In here." Julie called from the living room.

Anne plopped down next to Julie on the couch. "I know what I want to be when I grow up. I want to be a pastor. Can I invite some friends over after school tomorrow? I want to start teaching people about God."

"I guess that'd be okay."

"Yay!" Anne bounced up and down a couple of times on the seat cushion, before launching off the sofa and dashing back upstairs.

✧

Anne managed to convince two classmates to come to her house to learn about what the Bible *really said*. It hadn't been easy. She talked to ten acquaintances and most of them reacted to her invitation like she was asking them to come over and clean the toilet. But Sarah and Jody reluctantly agreed to listen to what she had to say.

She gestured for them to sit on the mattress in her room while she opened the Bible to a page she had selected the night before.

"Do you know what the word 'sin' means?" Anne asked.

"Sure, it means doing bad stuff," Sarah said.

"And not obeying the ten commandments," Jody said.

"Look at this." Anne held the opened book in front of them. "See that definition? It says, '*Miss the mark*.' That's it, that's all there is to it. It doesn't even mean doing bad things, it just means not doing the things you should be doing. It doesn't make you a bad person to miss the mark. It just means you messed up and need to get back on track. How cool is that?"

"Wow, that's really cool," Sarah said.

"So, not obeying the ten commandments would be a sin, because it misses the mark," Jody said matter-of-factly.

"Yes, it would. But it wouldn't make you an evil sinner or a bad person if you didn't obey them. It would just mean you were off track."

"Hmm," Jody said. "I don't know."

"What don't you know?"

"I'm not sure that I believe that it's just missing the mark."

"But that's the definition right here in the Bible."

"I know, but I'm still not sure."

Anne was confused by Jody's lack of enthusiasm about this new information. What was wrong with her? What was she afraid of?

"Okay, well look at this." Anne opened to another page and read.

> *"God is love, and whoever abides in love abides in God, and God abides in him."*

"See that, God is love. And when love is in us, God is in us. God isn't mean, God is love. Isn't that cool?"

"I like that," Sarah said.

"I like that too," Jody said. "What else did you find in there?"

Anne spent the next thirty minutes turning to different pages and sharing new ideas with the girls.

"Well, I've gotta get home," Sarah said.

"Me too," Jody said.

Anne smiled as she followed them to the door. *I can make a difference in the world. If people know who God really is, instead of the ugly things they've been told.*

"Okay. See you guys tomorrow."

☼

At the end of the service, Anne and her sister made their way down the aisle from their usual seat in the pew. It had been four Sundays since Anne got "saved" and started her own style of "Sunday School" at her home. Sarah and Jody were regulars. They helped recruit newbies to join them twice a week after school.

Julie told her that Pastor John had called last night and asked if Anne could stay after church to speak with him. Anne was certain that he'd heard about her gatherings and she was excited to talk with him about what was required to become a pastor.

"I'll be in the fellowship hall," Julie said.

"Okay." Anne sat down on the chair outside the pastor's office and watched as he finished greeting the last of the parishioners.

"Come in, Anne." Pastor John motioned for her to follow him into his office. She sat in the folding chair on the other side of his large metal desk.

"So, I hear you've been doing some Bible teaching at your house. Is that true?"

"Yep. And it's great. I've been able to help a bunch of friends understand the Bible better."

"Well, you need to stop. Only men are anointed to share the gospel. And if you continue to teach without the blessing and direction of God, you could hurt people."

Anne sunk in her chair. *Hurt people? How was she hurting people? She loved people and everything she was teaching was based on love.*

"I want to be a pastor." She looked at him to see if this made a difference. *Maybe if he knew how serious she was about teaching he would change his mind.*

"Anne, women can't be pastors. Only men have been chosen by God to instruct others. And when we do things outside of the will of God, we can do great harm to ourselves and the world. I need you to quit before you cause any more confusion than you already have. Do you understand?"

"Yes." Even though she wasn't sure she believed what the pastor was saying, she didn't want to hurt anyone.

✿

Her sister's hand-me-down couch sprung Anne upward with every buoyant-bounce of her petite twelve-year-old frame as she waited for Julie to finish vacuuming the living room for the party. Anne loved hanging out with her sister's friends. It made her feel like a grown-up. Last year, when Anne unwrapped the Malibu Barbie she'd been begging her mom to get her for her birthday, she quickly hid it under a pile of gift wrapping paper so that Julie wouldn't think she was childish.

As Julie put the vacuum in the hall closet, there was a knock at the door. Anne could see their step-brother Marvin's face through the crescent-shaped window in the door. She watched Julie walk across the living room to let the guys in. Marvin and his friends, Colby and Frank, had driven from California to Seattle for the Christmas holiday. Anne had met his friends once before when they visited last summer.

"Hi. Come in. It's great to see you," Julie said as she embraced Marvin.

The three young men made their way across the room where Marvin plopped down in the recliner and Frank found a place next to Anne on the couch.

"Oh, sorry, Colby, I'll grab a chair." Julie retrieved a chair from the kitchen.

Anne watched as Julie shifted in her seat, moving her long slender legs to an elegant angle that Anne thought looked like a movie-star pose. Anne adjusted her girlish legs to a similar position dangling from the couch. Last year Anne had experienced a growth spurt, shedding some of her baby fat and developing enough to proudly wear a training bra. She was taller than most of the girls in her class, but still shorter than the group in her sister's living room, ranging in age from 19 to 22 years old. All the guys looked like they had stepped out of an ad for California with their tan skin and blonde-to-brown windblown hair.

Anne continued to study Julie as she carried on a conversation with Marvin.

"So, Anne, are you ready to party tonight?" Frank asked.

Anne glanced up at Frank. "Um, sure." She shifted her body in an attempt to hide her uneasiness. She didn't think he was cute but she liked that an older guy seemed interested in her.

"What music do you like?" Frank said.

"Uh, mostly dance music, but, uh, I like a little bit of everything."

"Well, we're gonna have fun tonight. Maybe you'll dance with me?"

"Um, yeah, sure." Anne adjusted her body on the couch, moving her legs away from Frank.

"Do you like beer?" Frank asked.

"Uh, sure," Anne said, even though her only experience with alcohol was the time she was 10 years old and had a sip of her mom's wine.

"Well, I've got a half-rack of brewsky in the car that we can break into later."

Frank's crooked smile, which revealed his dimple and the mischievous look in his blue-gray eyes, made Anne feel like the prey of an animal that likes to play with its food.

☼

"Come on, chug that brewsky, Anne. You've been working on it for the last hour," Frank said.

Anne lifted the bottle to her lips and swallowed its remaining contents. Frank quickly opened and handed her another beer.

"Thank you," she said as she set the bottom of the bottle in her lap.

"Come on, take a drink," Frank said.

"I will, uh, in a minute … I have to go to the bathroom."

Anne took the beer into the bathroom and poured its contents down the sink and filled the bottle three-quarters full with water like she'd done with the previous two bottles. She returned to where Frank was waiting for her on the couch.

"So, Anne, have you ever been with a guy before?" Frank asked.

"Um, I'm not sure what you mean." Anne fidgeted and felt wary of where this was going.

"Oh, come on, you know what I mean … had sex? Have you ever had sex?"

"No." She wanted to run away before he had a chance to say what she sensed was coming next, but she was too inquisitive to move.

"You should let me be your first. I'll be super gentle, take it really slow with you. It'll hurt a little at first, but then you'll really like it. It'll feel really good.

Come on, let me be your first. We can go upstairs. I promise you'll like it."

Anne had checked out a book from the library about sex last year and had giggled with her friends at the descriptions of sexual intercourse, but she was still confused about how you actually do it. She wanted to know what it was all about. *How do you actually do it? What does it feel like?* But now, thinking about doing it for real, with this ugly guy that she barely knew, she wasn't sure why, but it seemed scary.

"I don't know." She panicked as her fear and curiosity competed for attention. No one had ever talked to her about sex, so she wasn't sure what she was supposed to feel about it, but it felt like a really big deal.

"It's better to let me be your first than someone who doesn't know what he's doing and won't take it slow with you. It'll be good for you and your future boyfriends. Just think about it."

Anne eyed the kitchen doorway as she rubbed the hem of her shirt between her fingers.

"If you take too long to decide you'll miss out on the time of your life."

Anne eased off the sofa and went to look for her sister. She wanted to be saved from this decision, which felt like something she could never take back. She walked into the kitchen and saw Julie standing by the fridge.

"Are you having fun?" Julie asked.

"Yeah. I have to ask you something," Anne said.

"Okay. Shoot."

"Frank wants me to have sex with him. He said he should be my first. Should I do it?" She hoped her sister wouldn't get too angry with Frank for suggesting it.

"Hmm … yeah, I think he'd be a good guy to be your first. He's really nice and I think he'd be very gentle with you."

Bewildered, Anne said, "Okay."

She thought, *why would Julie say that … why didn't she think it was a bad idea. I don't want her to think I'm a big baby, but, I don't even like this guy. Well, maybe Frank's right, maybe this will be good for me—at least Julie thinks so.*

She plodded back into the living room and approached Frank who was still seated on the couch.

"Okay," Anne said.

"Really? That's awesome. You won't regret it." Frank grabbed her hand and led her upstairs.

✧

She held back tears. With her clothes on again, she made her way down the stairs in search of comfort, in search of Julie. At the bottom of the staircase, Julie gazed over in her direction and the slow stream of anguish leaked from Anne's eyes. Yes, he had gone slow. Yes, he had been gentle. Yes, it was painful. But no, she didn't like it. She had wanted it to stop as soon as it began, but instead, remained silent and waited achingly for it to be over.

"How was it?" Julie said, as if asking about her day at school.

Anne wiped her hand under each of her eyes as the tears continued to well up.

"It was icky. I want to wash the dirty off."

"Oh, yeah, I felt that way too my first time. That's normal. Go ahead and shower, it'll help. I'll get you a towel."

There was a muffled quality to the world around her as Anne lugged her body to the bathroom.

She stood deathly still as the spray pounded her body. She had hoped a shower would remove the filth she felt deep beneath her skin. But, it was not helping. No amount of cleansing was going to wash away what happened.

✿

Anne - Today

I was raped.

Anne stared out the window of her apartment, as if outside was some distant universe.

It feels awkward to think that. I chose to have sex, so how can it be rape? But a child has no idea what they're agreeing to! The adults around me should've taken care of me. My sister should've protected me.

A tear slid down Anne's cheek.

It all makes sense now. When my sister told me that the creepy discomfort I felt was normal, that set the template for all my relationships going forward. That's why I've seen even the most hideous behavior in relationships as no big deal. You're supposed to feel uncomfortable. That's 'normal.'

She looked down at the paper that encapsulated her entire life on two pages. Two pages of tragedy and pain.

You poor girl. I'm so sorry. I've been so mean to you.

She cradled her cheeks, gave in to the sorrow, and wept.

GOOD JOB, ANNE.

The words boomed in her body.

Thank you, God.

Anne felt the compassion rush in like a flood.

I love me.

Given the crappy life I was dealt, I've overcome it all and still love everyone with reckless abandon. Everyone but me. Please forgive me. I'll take care of you from now on.

I promise.

ANNE,
DOMINIC
&
JOSIE

The Conversation

(Part Three - Six Months Later)

"How are ya?" Dominic said, as he and Josie sat across from Anne at the café where they met six months earlier.

"Good. Feeling mostly grounded," Anne said. "And, it's incredible, I haven't said one negative thing to myself in months. Not since I did that timeline exercise."

"Sweet, that's a good place," Dominic said. "I'm very excited for you right now."

"Thanks. It's so new to me and because I'm in the middle of it, it's difficult to feel excited. I just feel hopeful."

"Hopeful is the perfect place to be. I'm excited because I know where you're headed. I'm on the outside seeing all of it and it's beautiful."

"That's reassuring," Anne said. "I had this thought yesterday, that everything changes when we're able to see ourselves in the same compassionate way we see others, when they make mistakes or make poor choices in their lives. That until you fall in love with yourself, you'll never truly be happy."

"That's perfect," Josie said.

"I used to criticize myself all day long," Anne said. "Every idea, every action was met with the thought, *That's stupid,* or *What an idiot, what did you do that for?* I was so mean to myself. With the negative self-talk gone, I feel free to take actions where I felt stuck before."

"You *are* free and you like yourself," Josie said, enthusiastically.

"I love me." Anne smiled.

"How are your emotions?" Dominic said.

"I feel mostly balanced," Anne said. "The only thing that keeps coming up is the desire to be in a relationship with someone who sees my value and doesn't want anyone else. I still feel hurt about not being chosen by Derek. And those emotions continue to rear their ugly head."

"What you're feeling is normal. There's still some frustration and residue from that relationship. It'll pass," Dominic said.

"I hope so," Anne said. "I still have that yucky feeling of not being wanted."

"You're still taking it personally, but the ending was based on his inability to be a man," Dominic said.

"Why am I taking it personally? How do I stop? Is it healthy just to distract myself from this line of thinking? I'm so used to analyzing everything, I'm not sure when it's healthy and when it's not."

"You're an over-thinker," Dominic said. "You need to tell yourself it wasn't about you. He is a mess and yes, distract yourself and do something else. It wasn't you, he was a little boy."

"Okay, I'll work with that."

"You've come a long way and it's beautiful." Dominic smiled.

"I feel like people that see through the eyes of love are so rare that I may end up alone," Anne said. "I don't want to be in another emotionally vacant relationship. But when I look around me, that's the majority of what I see."

"It's true," Dominic said. "That's your past, but that's not who you'll be in relationships anymore. I can promise that. I see happiness in your future. Relationships that end that way, start hollow and you won't—"

"'Cause you're not hollow," finished Josie.

"Good point." Anne beamed.

"It's not just good, it's truth," Dominic said.

"You're right, it is truth. And truth is neither good or bad. It just is." Anne glanced at the message on her phone. "Do you remember that DNA test I sent in?"

"Yeah," Dominic said.

"When I viewed my results on Ancestry.com, there was a list of people that closely matched my DNA as family, and I sent a message to the five close matches this morning and one of them just responded."

"Really?" Dominic leaned closer. "What's the message say?"

"Hang on, let me read it." Anne opened the message on her phone. "Oh, my God."

"What?" Josie said.

"Could my mom have been telling the truth? Oh, my God." Anne stared at her phone.

"The truth about what?" Dominic urged.

"When I was about 8 years old, I asked my mom what my dad's name was and she told me it was Marcus Welby." Anne said. "I didn't believe her because it was a TV show. I thought she was just trying to hide his identity from me."

"That's funny," Dominic grinned.

"The person that just wrote me said one of their family surnames is Welby," Anne said.

"Wow. That's crazy," Josie said.

"I know," Anne said. "Hold on, I'm gonna write back."

Anne glanced up from her phone. "Where were we? Oh, yeah, I wanna be Derek's friend, but every time we talk, I keep trying to tell him how to fix things in his life," Anne said.

"Just be his friend, not a mom," Josie said.

"Ouch," Anne said.

"Derek is 15 years old, emotionally," Dominic said.

"Sounds about right. He lies to me to keep me from prying into his life. I know he's seeing someone else, even though he tells me she's *just a friend*. Not that it matters, but I don't know why he feels he has to lie about it. Is it healthy for me to stay friends with him?"

"Not with expectations," Dominic said.

"Is it wrong to expect honesty?" Anne said.

"Expecting honesty is okay from an emotionally healthy person but you can't expect it from a teenage boy that views anyone as an authority, that tells him how to live—and what do kids do to authority figures? They lie and hide stuff."

"Well, it doesn't seem like he gives a rip about me anyway. He never even said he was sorry for hurting me in New York," Anne said. "What's best for me? This is my biggest blind spot. When I care about someone, I can only see what's best for them."

"Your biggest challenge is backing away once you get involved," Dominic said.

"True, I don't know how to back off."

"That's why you push so hard," Dominic said.

"How do I back off?"

"By not needing to be heard," Josie said.

"So, I can still be his friend. I just need to let go of my need to be heard?"

"You care for people, which isn't bad, but it leaves you exposed," Dominic said.

"What do you mean, *exposed*?"

"You're so focused on the other person, you leave yourself open to get hurt," Josie said.

"I thought the whole point was to allow myself to be vulnerable and not worry about getting hurt?"

"True, but you stop caring for yourself to focus on someone else. Being vulnerable is about being seen and open. Not abandoning yourself," Josie said.

"So when I know someone will probably lie to me, do I continue to hang out with them and just let the need for honesty go, or do I stop hanging out with them?"

"Well, everyone lies in some fashion." Dominic said. "Why people feel the need to lie is based in fear of some sort. I don't take it personal."

"So at least for now, I need to think of Derek like I would a casual friend. Someone that I talk with on occasion, but not someone I get into deep conversations with."

"I think that's the way to go for now," Josie said.

"This makes me sad, but it feels like the right thing to –" Anne looked at her ringing phone and saw that Derek was calling. "Excuse me for a minute."

Anne returned to the table. "Okay. I know you said to back off with Derek, but he just called because he's upset about my post on Facebook about a guy. He's clearly jealous, even though I told him the guy is just a friend. He even said that he has no right to be jealous but then proceeded to say how it looked like I was throwing it in his face. I told him that the dude could be my son and I was commenting on his music. I don't know how to handle these situations. They don't come up often, but when they do, I feel the overwhelming need to talk him out of feeling insecure."

"I don't participate in manipulation," Dominic said.

"Is he manipulating me?"

"Of course he is," Josie said.

"I'm not sure that staying friends with him is the healthiest thing for me. He doesn't want a real relationship with me and he doesn't treat me like a *friend*. He goes on dates and calls it *just having coffee*. The lying sucks worse than the fact that he doesn't want to be in a relationship with me."

"That's the point. You need to do what's healthy for you," Josie said.

"I don't know what's healthy for me," Anne said. "He knows how I feel and he's been clear about where he's at, and I was fine to go along with it, I guess, sadly believing he would change his mind. I don't think we have anything left to say to each other on the topic of relationship. The problem is I'm in a relationship with him, pretending to be *just friends*, while he dates other women. Kind of messed up. But it works for him."

"You're *avoiding* the truth," Dominic said.

"Get out of your head, Anne. What do you *feel?*" Josie said.

"I feel resentful about making Derek a priority in my life when I'm clearly not a priority in his," Anne said. "Wow, it feels empowering to admit the truth. Less expectation."

"Absolutely," Dominic said.

"It's important we see people in an accurate way," Josie said.

"I feel freed from my self-imposed prison of stuckness," Anne said.

"When you're *all in* with what you *want*, you leave no room for anything else," Dominic said.

"Yep, I've been looking at all my options through the lens of *Derek doesn't want me, but he'll change his mind*," Anne said.

"We're only limited by ourselves," Dominic said. "How are you going to take care of Anne despite the shitty reality about Derek?"

"I don't know," Anne said.

"Make *yourself* the priority, Anne," Josie said. "Quit worrying about Derek, and take care of *you*. So what does self-care look like for you in this situation?"

"I don't know," Anne said. "Derek called me yesterday and during our conversation he mentioned how well he *gets me*. He then said, 'You poor thing, I am perfect for you.' So, I asked, 'But, I'm not perfect for you?' And he said, 'Maybe, but I can't say that for sure.' He keeps making comments about how awesome he is for me, and how sad it is for me that he doesn't want to be in a relationship with me. What am I supposed to do with that?"

"Tell him that you don't appreciate his asshole comments," Dominic said angrily.

"Dom." Josie gave him a look of disapproval.

"Well, it's emotional terrorism and not the way a friend behaves. It's like dangling candy in front of a kid, then slapping them for trying to grab it," Dominic retorted.

"He's right. You're not a toy for him to play with when he feels like it," Josie said.

"Well, if he ever decides to be with me, he's going to have some work to do to get me back," Anne said defiantly.

"That's how it should be," Josie said. "Whoever you end up with should pursue you. If they don't, then they aren't real men and aren't worth awesome Anne's time."

"Aw. Thanks, Josie."

"You need to concentrate on your own happiness, not anyone else's. You sometimes forget you're a badass chick." Dominic winked.

"Aw, thanks, you guys!" Anne said. "Putting *Anne* first for a change will be good for me, won't it?"

"Yep, you get lost in *why doesn't he want me, what's wrong with me.* When it should be, *what the hell is his problem? He's a dumbass for not wanting me,*" Dominic said.

"I like that." Anne giggled. "Derek's willing to crush me to serve his own agenda. I've given him a pass over and over again, making excuses for why he can get away with hurting me."

"That's why I keep using phrases like, *he's a dick, a douche, an asshole.* You need to see the truth despite emotion," Dominic said.

"I don't want any more dickhead men in my life," Anne said. "I'd rather be alone than be with a douche. Why on earth would I care if an asshole *wants* me? Why would I want to be wanted by an asshole? I want to be pursued and desired by someone who wants my best, as much as I want what's best for them. Derek doesn't care about what's best for me, he only cares about what's best for him."

"You go, girl!" Josie said.

"She replied," Anne said.

"Who?" Josie said.

"The person I emailed about the DNA test results," Anne said as she read the email on her phone. "Yes, they have a Marcus Welby in the family and he is about eighty years old now and yes, he lived in the Seattle area for a few years around the time my mom would've been pregnant with me."

"Holy shit, Anne," Dominic said.

"I know." Anne stared out the window at the cars driving by the café. "She said she's going to send some pictures later today."

"How exciting!" Josie said.

"Be sure and let us know what happens," Dominic said. "So, how's the dating going?"

"What? Oh, dating. Umm... I joined a dating site and it's fun to interact, but I haven't actually gone on a date yet," Anne said. "They keep falling through. The first guy I talked with decided to be exclusive with someone he had met before connecting with me, and the second guy just quit communicating. That's about it. So, I guess I'm enjoying the *idea* of dating."

"Well, keep putting yourself out there. It's good for you to have interactions with men other than Derek," Dominic said.

"When Derek and I talked on the phone yesterday, I told him, I'm dating," Anne said. "That I want to be in a relationship with a man that wants me. Derek reiterated that he doesn't want a relationship. That just hearing me talk about what I want reaffirmed what he doesn't want. I keep hoping he'll realize we belong together. Am I doing the right thing in moving on? I don't want to look back and regret my choices. I know he loves me and has been going a little crazy with jealousy at the thought of me dating, and now I basically told him he doesn't have to speculate, that *I am* dating and it's not just for the fun of it, that I want to be in a relationship with a man that adores me."

"You have to keep moving forward and stop having conversations with Derek," Dominic said. "You're giving him what he wants and not doing what's best for you."

"Okay. Just makes me sad. I think he's making a huge mistake in letting me go."

"You don't know the future and you can't *make* him do anything," Josie said.

"That sucks, but it helps." Anne said. "You don't think I've said anything to push him further away, do you? Or does it even matter?"

"If something you say can push him away, then you weren't that close to begin with," Dominic said. "You have to do whatever is necessary to distance the intimate connection you have with him."

"This is so hard!" Anne said. "I don't have firm boundaries with that man. I cave. Like tonight he invited me to hang out at his house and watch a movie, which would be fun, but what's implied in the invitation is that I will stay overnight. I'm exhausted from pretending everything is okay between us. It's time to be honest. God, this is gonna hurt."

"It's long overdue," Dominic said. "It's the reason you can't move on. You need to move on from Derek. You're falling into despair."

"I don't know how to do that."

"Stop communicating with him," Josie said. "He's stuck and you're stuck with him. I know it's hard, but just keep telling yourself why it's important."

"Endings have always been hard for me. Goodbyes, too."

"It's not goodbye, it's see you again, later," Josie said.

"Everything reminds me of him and I've been ignoring my feelings," Anne said.

"You're trying to control your emotions instead of grieving," Dominic said.

"Old habits die hard," Anne said.

"Gotta let it go," Josie said.

"I'm grieving the loss of what could've been," Anne said. "I don't want to want him. There are so many things I've seen in the last year that make me not even want to be his friend, but I can't seem to let go of him. I want him to want me, more than I actually want him. I think if he suddenly said, *Let's do this*, I'd be terrified."

"It's the *I hate it, but need it*, just like an addict," Dominic said.

"I have to stay away from the drug and breathe through the pain of withdrawal," Anne concluded.

"Exactly," Josie said.

Anne glanced at her phone. "Derek just texted with—"

"Put down the needle," Dominic said.

"Yes, sir," Anne bowed her head, like a scolded puppy. "I hate to admit it, but I'm wishing I'd never met Derek. I've never admitted regretting anything in my life. I usually put a positive spin on anything negative, and only see the good that came from it."

"That just means you're grieving in a healthy way," Dominic said.

"Hmm. Okay," Anne conceded.

"Be there, but don't stay there," Dominic said.

"Put down the needle." Anne laughed.

"Yes, you don't need it and you'll regret it. Instead thank God for the new direction," Dominic said.

"Talking to Derek won't change anything," Josie said. "The best thing you can do is to get and stay healthy and whole. Steer clear for a while of people that aren't on your home team. In other words, the people that don't benefit your life."

"Thank you both. You've helped so much."

"We're here for you anytime, Anne," Josie said.

"Yes, we are," Dominic agreed.

Anne, Josie and Dominic, reached the exit to the café and exchanged hugs goodbye.

"Stay in touch." Josie waved, as she and Dominic left the café.

"I will." Anne reached for her coat, hanging near the entrance. As she turned back to the door, she bumped into a tall, handsome, man, with dark brown hair.

"Oh, excuse me." The deep, soft, sound of his voice, made Anne feel like a nervous teenager.

"Um, no, excuse me." Anne stammered.

"Anne? It's Trent. Do you remember me? We met at the hospital several months ago." His wide grin revealed his dimple as he extended his hand towards Anne.

"Oh, my gosh! Yes, I remember you."

ANNE & TRENT

Real Freedom

The point where you love yourself more than anyone else is the point you are free to love everyone the right way. No more motives. Just love.

I watch Trent put my bag in the trunk of his car. It's been three months since we collided at the café. I'm eager for this trip, for our first weekend together. These last three months of cuddling, playful kisses, and late-night talks about hopes, dreams and the future—our future—have been pure bliss, like a fairy tale.

"You look so happy, Anne. I love that." Trent lightly strokes my cheek.

"I am happy. You're my dream come true." I lean over to the driver's seat and kiss his cheek.

"Aw, that's sweet." He takes my hand and gives it a squeeze. "You mean everything to me, Anne."

If anyone outside our world could hear the way we talk to each other, they would probably throw up a little. I know, because that used to be me. Now I crave all our cheesy little exchanges.

"I made something for you." He pushes a button on the car stereo.

A man's voice is singing—wait—

"Is that you?" I ask.

"Yes. Since the day I met you, this song has reminded me of you."

No music, just Trent's voice.
"Some say love, it is a hunger,
an endless aching need.
I say love, it is a flower
and you, it's only seed."

Here come the tears again. No one has ever done anything like this for me. I can't believe this beautiful gift of a man was brought into my life.

"Just remember in the winter, far beneath the bitter snow," his voice cracks a little as he finishes with *"Lies the seed that with the sun's love, in the spring becomes the rose."*

"I love you, Trent."

He turns his head and finds me watery-eyed, staring at him. He strokes my hand and smiles adoringly. "I love you too, Anne."

140

Trent hands me a glass of the Cabernet that we selected at the local grocery on the way here and pulls me next to him on the couch.

I nuzzle closer. "I want to melt into you."

"Aw." He wraps his arms around me and gives me a squeeze.

I gaze at the flames, dancing some sort of expressionist routine to the sound of the crackling logs. I take a deep breath. He lightly strokes my temple with his sturdy fingertips. I'm unexpectedly calm in his powerful embrace.

I trust him.

Trent gently leads me up the stairs. I'm holding his hand like a lost child as I follow him into the bedroom. I would follow him anywhere right now. He smells manly, a mixture of sweat and Aramis cologne and his grip is strong and kind.

He stops at the king-sized bed and draws me to him. I feel his excitement brush against my leg, as he lowers me onto the silky duvet.

He leans down and delicately kisses my lips, then pulls back and stares into my eyes.

"Are you okay with this?"

Huh? Of course, I am. Oh, wow, he'd actually stop without any argument, if I said *no*. I hold back tears. This is what it feels like to be loved.

"Yes." I barely get the response out.

He's undressing me, unhurriedly, deliberately. He takes off his clothes and looks at me.

"Is this okay? Are you okay?"

More than I've ever been in my life.

"Yes." I smile expectantly.

I've never cared about looking at a man's body. His naked body is beautiful lying next to me. I seem tiny, next to the muscular curve of his arm, which is the size of my thigh. His stocky legs are smooth and firm beneath my fingertips.

I want to feel him. I don't want to wait any longer. I roll to my side and fling my leg over his body to climb on top of him, but he pulls me back down to the bed. Why is he stopping me? Doesn't he want this?

"Not yet." The breathy growl of authority in his voice excites me as he softly sucks my bottom lip.

"I want you." I tug at his hip and try to bring him to me. He resists.

"I want you too, Anne, but I wanna take my time."

"You said my name." The words sound weird coming out of my mouth.

"Yes?" He looks confused.

"No one's ever said my name." I try to keep the moisture in my eyes from leaking.

"Oh, Anne. I'm so sorry." He holds me close and kisses my face.

"You know, for the first time *I'm here*."

"I do know."

At last. It feels good to succumb to the weight of his sturdy frame on top of me.

I can't think.
I'm not checked out. I'm fully *here*.
And it's the best feeling in the world.

ANNE

Taking Care of Me

I put the finishing touches on the pumpkin cake. His favorite. It's been six months since our first kiss. We've been inseparable since our trip to the ocean. In some ways, it feels like we've always been together. I've never been happier with a man. As a girl, I dreamed of a fairy-tale romance, but somewhere along the way I gave up the idea. Until Trent. He's changed everything.

He should be here any minute.
Candles, check. Wine, check. Love-note, check.
I hear the key turn in the lock.
"Happy Anniversary!" I run and wrap my arms around his neck. His arms are limp around my waist. Something's not right. I pull back and see the look of torment on his face.
"What's wrong?"
He grabs my hand and leads me to the couch.
"What's *wrong*?" I can hear the panic in my voice.

"Give me a minute."

Oh God. I'm so scared. Why isn't he saying anything? He won't even look at me.

"Umm."

Umm, what? Say it already.

"I've been thinking."

"Thinking about what?" Oh God, this can't be happening.

"Us."

"What? What does that mean?"

"Anne, please, just give me a minute."

"Okay, sorry." I hate it when he takes that tone.

"I need some space. This isn't working for me."

My heart is racing. I want to run. "What do you mean by space? What isn't working for you?" I'm impressed by the calmness in my voice.

"Everything is moving too quickly. I feel like we're already an old married couple."

"What's wrong with that?" I try to keep from sounding frustrated, but fail miserably.

"I'm not ready to settle down with the rest-of-my-life person. If I committed to you for forever, I know I'd eventually resent you, *unfairly*, for missing out on things I should've done, but didn't."

"What are you talking about? What things?"

"I don't really know. I just know I feel unsettled and like there are experiences I still need to have, before I commit to my lifetime person."

"Do you mean with other women?" I know that's exactly what he means, but I want him to admit it.

"I don't know. Maybe."

Bullshit, maybe. He knows that's exactly it. What the hell. I can't believe this.

"Really, maybe? You honestly don't know? Come on, be specific."

"Okay, I want to date other women," Trent says. "But, we can still see each other. I just need to be single for a while. You know, when I met you, I'd just ended another relationship. I didn't give myself any time alone, before jumping into a relationship with you ..."

My focus drifts. I know he's still talking, but I no longer hear him. He's right. I'm the rebound girl. There's no point resisting. All endings need space before new beginnings. I know this. I had hoped we were the exception to the rule.

I don't want to be friends. I can't be *friends*. It's time to move on.

It's time to take care of *me*.

ANNE

Dad

Anne boarded the Airbus A321 for North Carolina, where her healthy, energetic 80-year-old dad lived. Just two weeks ago, she'd stared at her phone as the incoming call displayed an unfamiliar number, location *Marion, North Carolina.* She'd answered, hoping for the best, but bracing for the worst. He could say he didn't know her mom. He could deny he was her father. Instead, after he received her letter and the carefully selected photographs of Anne now and as a baby with her mom, his first pained words to his newly discovered daughter were, "Why didn't your mom tell me about you?"

Anne placed her luggage in the overhead bin and took her aisle seat.

"Is Charlotte your final stop?" asked the woman next to the window in Anne's row.

"No, I catch another flight in Charlotte to Asheville," Anne said.

"Oh, Asheville is beautiful. Have you been there before?"

"No, I'm going to meet my father for the first time." Anne smiled.

"What? How exciting! A friend of mine just found her father too, after 20 years of searching."

"I'm super excited." Anne said. "It's kinda crazy. I've always thought that genetic family wasn't important, that it's better to choose your family. And now, I'm on my way to meet the man who contributed to my existence and he wants a relationship with me. I feel grounded for the first time in my life. I feel like I belong, like I'm finally a *real* person. Isn't that weird?"

"I completely under—"

"Excuse me," said the tall, slender, young woman pointing at the middle seat in Anne's row.

"Would one of you mind trading seats with me, so that we can sit together?" asked the tall young man standing next to her.

"Where's your seat located, honey?" said the woman next to the window.

"There." The man pointed at a seat one row back on the aisle.

"Sure, I'll trade ya."

The man took his new seat next to the window. The young woman in the seat between him and Anne, put her head in her hands, while he rubbed her back. "It's okay. I'm here."

"What's wrong? Are you okay?" asked Anne.

"Oh, she's afraid of flying. She hasn't been on a plane before," said the man.

"Oh," Anne said. "Well, you're gonna be fine, sweetie. There's nothing to be afraid of. I fly all the time."

Anne leaned back in her seat and listened to music as the plane climbed to reach its cruising altitude. She was on her way to meet her father. It still felt like a dream. A dream she never knew she could have—

"This is your captain," said the voice from the cockpit. "We've experienced an anomaly in one of the engines and we're going to have to head back to the airport."

Anne thought they'd leveled off quicker than usual. Her mind raced with frustration. *Why is this happening? I don't want to wait any longer to meet my dad. I've waited my entire life! This sucks.*

The girl next to her was trembling and the man with her attempted to console her.

"This is your flight crew," said the voice over the intercom. "We need to prepare for an emergency landing. Please review the procedures in the back of your seat pocket."

Shrieking, sobbing, and whimpering pervaded the cabin as the flight attendants made their way down the aisle, assisting passengers with the mechanics of preparing for a crash landing.

"Please practice, bracing for impact," said the voice over the intercom. "When we say, 'brace for impact' be prepared with one of the methods shown in your instructions."

The woman next to Anne was howling and shaking uncontrollably.

149

"Don't take any of your belongings with you during the emergency evacuation," continued the voice of a flight attendant. "I repeat, leave all of your belongings behind."

The chaos of sound around Anne transformed into background noise.

I can't believe this. After all these years, I finally, unbelievably, find my father. A father who is still alive and wants a relationship with me! And I'm going to die on a fucking plane on my way to meet him. Is this some kind of cruel joke?

Fifteen minutes later, applause and cheering erupted, as the wheels of the plane smoothly and miraculously touched down on the airport runway.

"We'll wait on the tarmac for the brakes to cool down," said the voice over the intercom, "and we'll approach the gate when it is safe to do so. I'd like to thank my co-pilot for landing us safely."

Cheers and applause filled the cabin again.

After three hours of phone calls to various airlines, Anne boarded another plane to meet her dad.

She gazed out the window. *I could've died today. I've been so busy feeling angry that it never occurred to me to be scared. All I feel is relief. Relief, that I'm now finally on my way to meet my dad. Knowing he exists has changed me. I feel grounded and at peace. I was searching for my dad all along, in every past relationship. Wow. I was trying to get something from those men that only having a dad could provide.*

Anne scanned the regional airport corridor for her newly discovered family. As she approached the baggage claim area, she saw a man smiling and walking toward her. It was him. The man she never knew. Who never knew she existed. The man who not only was her father, but *wanted* to be her father.

He got closer, and his eyes were familiar to Anne, like looking in a mirror. This was *her* father. She was a *real* girl. She felt *complete* as she leaned into his outstretched arms and tears streamed down her face.

ANNE, DOMINIC & JOSIE
The Conversation

(A Year Later)

"When I think back to my time in NYC, the pain is minimal in comparison to the overwhelming sense of empowerment I feel now," Anne said.

"That's great, Anne," Josie said.

"Overall, I'm at peace," Anne continued. "I don't feel the extreme highs and lows that I used to feel. Now when I feel sad, it's just sadness ... not debilitating."

"That's what balance feels like. It has little ups and downs," Dominic said. "We all like the high better, but when we are balanced emotionally, we have peace and we see the world clearer."

"I've noticed that," Anne said. "Ya know, I no longer feel the need to be in a relationship. Ever since my breakup with Trent last year, followed by finding my father, whenever my thoughts drift to having a boyfriend, I remember the pain that can come with that, and how fulfilled I am right now, with *me*."

"That's a great place to be, Anne," Josie said.

"I've learned life is about being fearless in your honesty with yourself and God," Anne said. "I'm afraid of many things, but I will not be afraid to be honest and true to myself. Sometimes it just takes a minute for me to catch up with my emotions and remember that. I have compassion for myself and I talk to myself the way I would comfort a child. When I'm anxious, I remind myself, 'Don't struggle.'"

"That's beautiful, Anne," Josie said.

"Everyone has an inner guidance system, which nudges them to move toward what feels light and let go of what feels heavy," Dominic said.

"When my relationship with Trent ended, that's how I knew I couldn't be his friend while he pursued being single," Anne said. "Because when I imagined it, I felt tremendous heaviness, where the thought about ending it completely, while excruciatingly painful, felt *right*. There was a sense of peace that came with letting him go. And now, I pay attention to this *knowing*, regularly."

"I'm so proud of you, Anne," Dominic said. "It's an honor to be on this journey with you."

"Seriously. Thank you, both, for being voices of truth for me," Anne said. "Nothing cuts through the crappy emotions quicker than the truth of *what's so*. It shifts everything, and then it just takes a short time for the emotions to catch up. I'm feeling balanced, happy and at peace!"

"I love truth," Dominic said.

"I'm so happy for you, Anne," Josie said.

"Me too. Truth is a miracle worker." Anne said. "We must never let fear turn us against our playful hearts. So many of us choose our path out of fear, disguised as practicality. Don't get me wrong, I'm still responsible. But everything doesn't have to be *practical*."

"Yep, it's okay to have *fun*," Josie, teased.

"I know that now," Anne said. "As T.D. Jakes says, you need to '*Enjoy your relationship with yourself, and then anybody else that comes in, enters into a party you already started.*'"

"That's awesome!" Josie laughed.

"What's next for you?" Dominic said.

"Everything is coming together, Dominic," Anne said. "I have an amazing and loving new family that I'm getting to know. Not only did I find my dad, who loves me already, but I have a sister that is so much like me, it's as if we grew up together. I'm going to be splitting my time between the west coast and east coast to make sure I don't miss out on any more life with my dad and sister. I'm doing some dating and enjoying it without any compulsion to rush into a relationship. And I let a friend of mine read some of what I wrote this last year and she wants to publish it as a book. I'm happy and truly at peace for the first time in my life."

"Something will grow from all you are going through. And it will be you!"

From Jason

I've learned so much in my life and some of it has been difficult to deal with at times. But I'm immensely thankful for it all. I went through an amazing transformation and it's left me happy and thankful to be me for the first time in my life. I've learned that when I love myself and see myself for who I really am, then I'm able to love others and see the real person behind the mask. I now see women as special and priceless, not as toys to be discarded when I'm through with them.

Desiree (aka "Josie") asked me once, Jason, why don't you fight for our friendship? This pissed me off at the time, but not long afterwards I saw she was right. I'd become lazy and defeated. I didn't fight for anything. I'd given up. I had to show her I could fight. She needed to see me clawing my way out of the depression and depravity that had become who I was. It took time, but now she knows me as a fighter who doesn't quit. She knows I want to live life to its fullest and I love being me every day.

Life is beautiful today and not because it's without problems. But problems don't overtake me anymore. When you settle into being who you're supposed to be, it is freeing and gives you confidence to go through any trial or struggle.

For me the happiest and most amazing moment was when Desiree said she would be my wife. She's always loved me, but I became the guy of her dreams and that woman makes me crazy to this day. She pushes buttons I didn't know I had. But she is my best friend and loving myself gave me the ability to accept her love and love her back.

If I can change, anyone can change. I've lived a hard life. I grew up poor, abused, and neglected, and it changed me into a self-centered, dreamless player. I've been transformed into a people-lover who will sacrifice anything to help someone and who is completely in love and committed to one woman and will not stop chasing my dreams.

I've traveled to the deepest parts of me and it gave me a passion for helping others. I didn't know what I would do with that passion until I saw a book entitled, *Life Coaching for Dummies*. I remember the first person I helped and everyone since then, totaling 643 people to date, including Anne. I don't use the number to brag in any way. I use it to show that one guy that took hold of his future and fought for himself has made a difference by helping people.

Imagine if you did the same?

No matter who you are or how you live, you can have the life you dream of. You can be who you really want to be and, most importantly, you can love the person in the mirror.

My transformation was trial and error. It wasn't easy, but it was so worth it. I would do it all over again. I hope you, too, will take the journey to a whole and healthy life. You can travel the world and you won't find the peace that is already inside you, just waiting for you to fight for it.

Thank you for reading. I hope you find the help you need in this book and know that I completely believe in you.

-Jason (aka "Dominic")

Loving yourself…does not mean being self-absorbed or narcissistic, or disregarding others. Rather it means welcoming yourself as the most honored guest in your own heart, a guest worthy of respect, a lovable companion."

-Margot Anand

From Anne

I love me. This has not always been the case. Most of my adult life, I've loved everyone but me with reckless abandon, and often to the detriment of my health and wellbeing. I'm fiercely loyal and I don't "fall out of love." Once I love you, I will love you forever. It's just who I am. Unfortunately, I didn't have this same love and compassion for myself until recently. A devastating breakup, combined with isolation in an unfamiliar city, provided the perfect storm to crack the armor I'd built up over a lifetime to protect myself from pain. The first step for me was allowing myself to simply feel the pain. This was excruciating. At times, it felt like it would never end. But with each day the pain lessened and the joy began to appear.

There were two main factors holding me back from loving myself and living the life I was meant to live. One factor was perceiving being raped at age twelve as a good thing and no big deal, believing I was in control and made the choice. Once I recognized the truth of this event in my life, it changed everything for me. I saw how it had set the template for all my romantic relationships going forward. I believed that it was normal to feel uncomfortable in relationship and tolerated all behavior that made me uncomfortable.

The second factor was not having a father in my life. I was emotionally a lost little girl, looking for her father in all her romantic relationships. Finding my father changed this for me. I realized that it didn't even matter if he wanted me in his life at this point. Just knowing that I had a father, that I had a connection in this world, roots, gave me peace and eliminated the longing to find my father in the men I dated.

The last two years of my life have been life-changing. And Jason has been instrumental in this transformation. The steps he walked me through are the same steps we've provided in this book and my hope is that you will follow them and have your own breakthrough, finding the happiness and freedom you deserve.

Thanks for reading my story. I truly hope it has cracked *your* armor and begun a process for you that will lead to health, happiness, wellbeing and freedom.

-Dayna (aka "Anne")

✿ THE TOOLS

For Your Own Self-Discovery

Tools for Your Own Journey

You've now read Dominic and Anne's stories, and while you may or may not have a similar story, the hope is that you can relate to the way that they viewed the world, how they functioned because of the trauma they each suffered as children, or that you can see their transformations and that you desire a shift in your life.

Trauma is defined as a deeply distressing or disturbing experience that alters the way you see the world around you and the way you live your life. After reading about Anne and Dominic's transformations, you may ask, how does this help me or how can I have my own transformation? While we can't promise that life will instantly get better and all your dreams will come true, we can promise that if you allow them, the tools in this book can give you hope that life can get better. Each day that you practice them, you can move towards experiencing more happiness and peace in your life than ever before.

Are We There Yet?

How long will this process take? The answer is, it depends on *you* and that's the truth. It takes an average of 21 days to adjust to or form a new habit and that's what this process is designed to do. To make a habit of loving yourself and looking forward to your future and dreams.

This process relies on you, which means, you can do it in as little as 60 to 90 days or you can take your time. It just depends on you, your personality and your past.

Don't get stuck on how long it will take. If you focus on that, you won't notice the little changes. Your success can't be measured in time. Success can only be measured in changes you see in yourself. You just need to focus on being consistent. Keep the momentum moving forward and before you know it, you will see a difference. Don't try and rush this process. You need the changes to be real and lasting. Take as much time as you need. You are worth it.

We've included a suggested timeline. This is simply a guideline. Trust yourself to know the best pace for you.

Suggested Timeline

DAY 1:

Make the decision to start this process.

WEEK 1:

Complete the "The Thinker, The Feeler, The Doer" section and test. Spend a couple of days observing yourself and your behavior as it relates to your temperament.

NEXT 30 DAYS:

Complete the "Time to Clean My Glasses" and "Keep the Change" sections. This is where the habit of treating yourself well is learned. This process needs 30 days to become habit.

NEXT 30 DAYS:

Start the "Their Side of the Field" section. Take a week to determine your teams. In addition, keep doing what's working from the last 30 days. Once you've decided who's on your Home team, it's time to take the journey deeper and begin the "Whoa That's Deep" section.

TO INFINITY AND BEYOND:

Now it's time to begin the "Eyes Forward" and "Dream a Little Dream" sections. These are steps Anne and Dominic still walk today. So, once you start them they will be important forever.

This timeline is just a suggestion. You may take longer or get through it sooner. There isn't a right or wrong timeframe. Just keep moving. If you feel stuck, feel free to email us and we will do our best to help:

email: **IJTIM.questions@gmail.com**

Let's Get Started!

These tools are provided to guide you through a process similar to what Jason and Dayna used, so that you may enjoy a balanced life, too.

Important to this process is understanding your uniqueness. Specifically, why you think, feel, and respond the way you do ...

The Thinker,
The Feeler,
The Doer

To begin, we want to determine your temperament or personality type. Are you a *Thinker*, a *Feeler*, or a *Doer*? Understanding your temperament will allow you to see yourself and others more clearly. It's possibly the most important tool in this book and with it you may unlock a whole new future.

The Test

This test is designed to give you a better understanding of yourself. Choose the answer that applies to the behavior you've experienced *most frequently*, not the one you wish were true. There are no right or wrong answers and the three personalities are of equal importance and equal value. Answer each question according to who you are today and have been in the past. This will help obtain the most accurate result. Also, your first answer is typically the truest one. Pick only one answer for each question. Once you've answered all the questions, count how many of each letter you've chosen. The letter with the highest count is your dominant type.

1. When I'm alone …
    a. I need to get stuff done.
    b. I'm at peace.
    c. I need to find someone to hang out with.

2. At a party …
    a. I'm the center of attention and usually loud.
    b. I prefer to sit quietly and observe.
    c. I focus on the needs of other people.

3. My job is …
    a. Never good enough. I need a better one.
    b. Comfortable. Even if I don't like it, I'll keep doing it.
    c. I change jobs often and not always for the better.

4. When I need to make a decision, I …
    a. Make it quickly.
    b. Weigh all the options before making it.
    c. It depends on how I feel.

5. When I'm stressed …
    a. I pace and cuss.
    b. I retreat to my thoughts.
    c. I cry.

6. My friends see me as ...
    a. Having a lot of irons in the fire.
    b. Quiet and possibly withdrawn.
    c. Fickle or flighty.

7. When I dream ...
    a. I see my dreams as attainable.
    b. I need to know that my dreams are attainable.
    c. I change my dreams often.

8. Under pressure I ...
    a. Blame others.
    b. Become critical of others and myself.
    c. Take the blame and withdraw.

9. When I cry, I cry ...
    a. I don't cry. Crying is for sissies.
    b. Alone. It's likely that no one knows.
    c. Anywhere, anytime, and in front of anyone.

10. Which person from history do you relate to most ... (You don't have to like this person, just identify with them more than the others.) ...
    a. Oprah Winfrey
    b. Albert Einstein
    c. Ellen Degeneres

Now, add up your answers. (How many A's, B's and C's did you choose?)

A _____

B _____

C _____

If you answered mostly A's, your temperament is that of a Doer.

If you answered mostly B's, your temperament is that of a Thinker.

If you answered mostly C's, your temperament is that of a Feeler.

Next, find and read through the description of the basic characteristics for your type. The description isn't exhaustive. It's simply a baseline to help you understand yourself better.

"It has been my observation that the happiest of people, the vibrant doers of the world, are almost always those who are using—who are putting into play, calling upon, depending upon—the greatest number of their God-given talents and capabilities."
-John Glenn

The Doer

Doers are strong-willed, easily bored, extremely energetic, dream sellers who don't care about facts. It's only the goal that matters to them. Doers have a tendency to distort reality. They accomplish the task through people, and these people are tools to be used until broken. They enjoy retelling the story where they are the hero; such as the football game in which they threw the winning touchdown.

The Doer thrives in conflict. They often pick fights to break up boredom and are often out of touch with others' feelings. Doers are very creative and can typically respond to any problem quickly. They are not easily discouraged and do not see obstacles. Doers are beasts in a good way. They can climb any mountain and accomplish anything they decide to do. They cannot sit still and always have a lot of irons in the fire. They make great salesmen and are great at getting others to hop aboard their dreams. They are born to lead and can't play second fiddle to anyone easily.

They have brought about some of history's greatest victories and accomplishments. Doers have been responsible for horrible tragedies like the Holocaust, but they have also helped free entire countries and fed billions of people. There have been great and horrible Doers in history.

Some of the famous ones are:
Mahatma Ghandi, Martin Luther King, Hitler, Nelson Mandela, Oprah Winfrey, Barack Obama, Donald Trump and Dominic from this book.

"Never hide things from hardcore thinkers. They get more aggravated, more provoked by confusion than the most painful truths."

-Criss Jami

The Thinker

Much of what characterizes the *Thinker* is explained in the name. Thinkers experience all aspects of life in their head. Everything is a thought process. They are fiercely loyal perfectionists that value truth and honesty above all else and because they put such a high price on truth and honesty, they expect everyone else to do so as well. This is why lying to them crushes them. They can handle a painful truth over a little white lie.

They are analytical and sometimes pessimistic. They know all that is wrong with them and every weakness they have. They must always have something to think about and are often quiet. Their quietness is sometimes mistaken for anger or disinterest, but they really are just thinking.

Thinkers have high anxiety and fear of the unknown and find security in money. Others are drawn to thinkers because they are highly intelligent, serious, and they live by high standards. They are responsible for many breakthroughs in our society throughout history.

Here is a list of some of the famous ones:

Leonardo da Vinci, Sir Isaac Newton, Plato, Nikola Tesla, Albert Einstein, and this story's Anne.

*"Some are afraid of being a mess, feared by the unknown and are horrified by an unplanned future; then there are some of us who thrive through discovery, excited by unknown territories and intrigued by a future of mystery. How you tell these people apart; one is a thinker, the other a **feeler**."*

-*Nikki Rowe*

The Feeler

What can we say about the feeler? Well, whatever we do say we must say it nicely because they are easily crushed by negativity. Feelers value relationship above all else. Relationships equal identity with them. If you visit a feeler in their home, you will be given the royal treatment and their family will get left out while they focus on you.

We all have people in our lives who process life through emotion. They take in everything through a grid of emotion. They are impulsive and distracted by the next shiny thing. They will often follow the morals of the crowd. They have short-term memory when it comes to shortcomings in others. They allow others to fail them over and over and often take the blame for the failure of others.

They are not above using manipulation to get their way. Feelers love hugs. If you hug them ten times, they want one more. They are enthusiastic and have no problem expressing their feelings freely. Their emotions will bounce up and down quickly or build up pressure, which is what makes them the most creative people. They are artists, musicians, and often religious. Feelers are the heart of the world. They love deeply and are empathetic beyond what should be possible. They make the world beautiful with love and color and sound.

Some of the famous ones are:

Angelina Jolie, Joel Osteen, John Lennon, Picasso, Michelangelo and this story's Josie.

"We see the world through the lens of all our experiences; that is a fundamental part of the human condition."
                                        -Madeleine M. Kunin

Time to Clean My Glasses

Sometimes in order to get where we want to go, we have to revisit where we've been. In both stories, there was a point where Dominic and Anne each recognized for the first time that the abuse they suffered as children was *abuse*. Neither of them saw the tragedy of their situations, and these events defined how they saw themselves and everyone around them for much of their lives.

Dominic had convinced himself growing up that his repeated sexual abuse was a trophy to brag about to the guys. The guys would pat him on the back like he was some kind of hero, because he had sex before anyone else. What he couldn't see was the trail of destruction he left everywhere. Many undeserving women were sex objects to him. His distorted perception of life left him empty and insecure.

All of this changed in a moment when he was forced to face the truth by people who loved him and that little boy inside him that demanded some level of justice. Dominic had two emotionally challenging days that allowed him to see the little boy face to face and relive the horrors that happened to him at the hands of two predators. This was a defining moment for him. For the first time, he saw through fresh lenses as he wiped the tears away. He clearly saw his truth. He no longer saw a trophy to hoist above his head to

174

proclaim his victory over women. He saw tragedy and his innocence that had been taken. This changed him forever. He was finally able to mourn his loss and start living the way he had always dreamed about.

It all began with seeing the truth.

Most people have endured something in their life that they didn't see the truth of at the time. When this misperception is left unchecked, the cycle and damaging view of ourselves continues throughout our life.

Let's begin to change that now. The process of getting to the point where you value yourself above all else is simple but it isn't easy. For Anne and Dominic this change in perspective was freeing.

Take Action

To begin, you need a pen, paper, a couple of hours of alone time, and most of all, the willingness to revisit your past with honesty. Anne and Dominic revisited their pasts and saw the abuse for what it truly was, and while this may seem like a no-brainer to some, the challenge is that we often change the meaning of events to try and get through them without falling apart. In order to maintain the lie, if you continue, day after day, to reinforce the false meaning, you push the truth to a deep place. The lie then festers until you can't take it anymore and you fall apart, or you begin to punish yourself.

This process of reinforcing a false belief about a traumatic event is not exclusive to sexual abuse. It can happen for many reasons, including but not limited to, abandonment, bullying, emotional or physical abuse.

Let's get started. It's best to go somewhere in nature. If you can't, then choose a place where you won't be interrupted. You'll replay the mental movies stored in your mind. Starting from your childhood to today, revisit the significant events—meaning significant to you—in your life.

On your paper make three separate columns.

The first column is <u>Age.</u> How old were you when the event occurred?

The second column is <u>Event.</u> What was the event? Write a short sentence summarizing what happened.

The third column is <u>Feelings.</u> How did you feel when it happened? Write a couple of feeling words to describe what you felt.

Anne thought it was normal as a young girl to be handed over to an adult for sex. Dominic thought it was cool to be repeatedly molested by babysitters. Their whole lives changed when they saw the truth of how traumatic these events actually were.

What truth is waiting inside you to be seen? It may be painful to revisit it but the truth is designed to crush us and then build us back up to true peace and freedom. You only have pain to lose and clean lenses to gain.

"Your life does not get better by chance, it gets better by change."
                                                            -Jim Rohn

Keep the Change

Change is terrifying. The mere idea of it ushers in a million thoughts and fears. The questions fire off in our heads one by one as we duck to miss them because pursuing change is always a step completely into the unknown. As you read the stories, you can see both characters were completely stuck in cycles that led to sadness and frustration. Perhaps the most difficult part of change is that you have to have faith in the one person you haven't been able to trust; the one person whose fault it is for who you are today. Yourself.

We often see the areas *other* people struggle with better than our own. We see the changes *they* could make to greatly improve *their* life. Anne could see the things Dominic needed to change easily, but couldn't see the same shortcomings in her own life. Once she saw how her past experiences affected her, the desire to change was stirred up in her and she started taking little steps towards big changes, beginning with changing the way she saw herself. And for the first time she saw herself as valuable.

Everyone lives life according to the value they believe they have. This means that if you see yourself as not good enough, you will accept or allow others to treat you poorly, and believe you deserve it. Allowing others to treat you poorly, time and time again, damages you a little bit more every time it happens. Anne and Dominic took charge of their lives and forever changed the way they thought, the way they saw themselves and life around them. Most of all the way they lived.

This isn't something exclusive to them. You can experience the same thing with a little desire and willingness to try something different. The rest of this chapter includes some simple, potentially life-changing steps to help alter today, tomorrow, and the future. These are the same steps that Anne and Dominic used to change how they lived. Try them for 30 days. The time is going to go by whether you try them or not, at least this way you will be taking back control of your health and wellbeing.

Take Action

Change the behavior. Change the life!

Start small. You don't want to make drastic changes based on emotion. The changes never stick because they are not maintainable. However, if you start with easier, realistic changes you will find yourself able to celebrate accomplishments daily.

We believe the following order is best; however, you know yourself better than we do. The goal is to just get moving.

- Start each day speaking positively to yourself, not on social media or watching TV. How you start the day sets the pace for the rest of the day, so speak kind words to yourself. Tell yourself even if you don't believe it yet that you are able to accomplish your dreams and goals. It will make a difference if you believe in yourself.

- Be honest with yourself about what you feel and think. Start a journal. Write what you think or feel for five minutes, increasing the time as you are able.

- Exercise for 30 minutes. Find the kind of exercise that suits you. If you're uncertain, you can start by taking a walk, but get into motion. You need to show yourself that you matter and release the good chemicals that come from movement.

- Change the way you eat. If you eat too much, try less. If you eat junk food, eat some healthy food instead. But alter your eating habits in some small way and increase the changes as you feel better.

- See a doctor. Especially if you have an illness or injury. Often, we let things go because we are in some way punishing ourselves or just haven't cared enough about ourselves. At the least, get a physical.

- Try something new. Either learn something new or visit somewhere new. You deserve an amazing life, but you are the only one who can give yourself that.

- Accept that sometimes life goes differently than planned. Learn to adjust. Don't allow a setback in your plans stop you. Keep moving forward.

- Be grateful for everything. We can get so lost and frustrated that we forget to be thankful for the beautiful parts of life all around us. Create a habit of seeing the beauty that's everywhere. One way to do this is to search it out and take a picture of the things you see that are either beautiful or encouraging and write about why they are beautiful. Do this once a day for 30 days and you will see life differently.

- Most importantly, give yourself permission to grieve the pain and loss you feel right now. You may have a lot of unhealed emotional and/or mental wounds that you still need to cry about to mourn the loss or pain from something or someone. Let it out.

- Allow people to give you compliments and praise. Accept the gift of love from others. Also, allow yourself to laugh often, including laughing at yourself. It heals you in many ways. It's okay to enjoy yourself.

- Finally, the most important thing is to get moving. Break your routine and learn new things about yourself. Try as many of these as you can. But, just get moving!

"Some of the most poisonous people come disguised as friends and family. You cannot expect to live a positive life if you hang with negative people."

-*Joel Osteen*

Their Side of the Field!

We are up 21 to 7 on a beautiful fall day as we sit here, cheering for our home team during our annual homecoming game. As the quarterback throws a long touchdown pass, everyone sitting in the bleachers with me leaps to their feet, cheering, high-fiving and hugging. They kick the extra point to lead by 3 touchdowns with 4 minutes left in the game. We all sit back down, basking in our impending victory. As it gets quiet, a man in the fifth row yells, "Clayton, you suck!" Not sure that I heard him accurately, so I ignored it. But then the loud, clearly drunk man said it again and made demeaning comments about Clayton's mom.

Clayton was our star quarterback, and this time the anger of the entire group of people turned on his heckler. They told him to *go to hell* but he only got more belligerent. Just when it looked as though it was going to get much worse, security came to take him and his wife away, saving him from what was sure to be a beating and his wife from seeing it happen. You never mess with the small-town quarterback. He's a hero.

The heckler was in disguise. He was wearing our school colors and sitting on our side of the field. No one would have guessed that he was the enemy. He was hiding in plain sight.

From the other side of the field, you could see him, still yelling, though now he was too far away to affect us anymore.

Right now, in your life there are covert douchebags who smile while they belittle, degrade, or dismantle you altogether. They always have something negative to say, and they do so while saying they care about you. Virtually every time you're around them, you leave feeling crappy. The hard part is that often these people are the people we are dating or are our brothers, sisters, uncles, aunts, or even our moms and dads. Sometimes these people have been lifelong friends.

We let them treat us horribly and we chalk it up to *that's just the way they are*, even though they have left us feeling and thinking that we are worthless time and time again. No matter what you say, they have a way of spinning it in a negative direction. They suck all positives out of our life.

Dominic recognized that most of the people in Anne's life were uncaring and unsupportive of her. She had grown so accustomed to the weight of these relationships she had no idea how damaging they were to her. Many of us have relationships that don't add value to our lives. When Dom brought this to Anne's attention, this truth broke her heart but it was also a revelation for her. Why did she hang out with and talk to people who were so negative? After all, shouldn't friends and family build you up and encourage you? Dominic got Anne to make a list, separating the people in her life into two columns: <u>Home</u> team and <u>Away</u> team. She then began grossly limiting for 30 days the time she spent with anyone on the *Away* team. This opened her eyes greatly, and every day she grew more comfortable with herself. She transformed into a confident person who saw a brighter future.

We give you the same challenge. We know it's not the easiest thing to do, but we also know that it works 100% of the time. When you surround yourself with supportive and encouraging people, it greatly improves your life in almost every way, including your outlook.

Take Action

Sit in a quiet place. Divide a piece of paper into two columns.

The first column is your <u>Home team.</u> These people are positive. They build you up, and are truthful with you at all costs. They are your cheerleaders, not backstabbers. Your home team people do not drain you. They make you laugh and are always actively trying to help you win, grow, and succeed. They make your life better just because you know them.

The second column is the <u>Away team.</u> Oh, where to start with them. Well, they are all-around negative people. They are only interested in criticism, put-downs and judgment. They suck the life out of the people in their lives and to have to talk to them is dreadful. You often question why you are friends and if they really care. They leave you feeling like crap.

There may be some people that you're not sure which column they belong in. Maybe you haven't spent enough time with them to know, because you've been spending all your time with your Away team. For these people, you can make a third column titled "Unsure" and put those people in this column for now. At the end of spending thirty days with your Home team, you can take a closer look at the *unsure* column and decide if you want to spend time with any of them to determine which team, Home or Away, they belong on.

In making the list, you must be truthful. Sometimes family is on the Away team. We often give people a pass because they are family. However, if they were *close* family they would act like it and treat you in a loving manner.

This will work only if you're honest with yourself. This isn't about writing people off. That's not the goal. You don't have to end relationships with people who are on your Away team. It's simply about choosing who you spend your time with.

So. after you've completed the list, for the next 30 days, spend time with only people on your Home team. In doing so, you will limit the negative influences in your life.

It's also very important for you to show yourself that you care for yourself above all else. That may sound silly, but when you hang out with negative people out of obligation, you place what's good for you, behind everyone else's needs and this doesn't benefit anyone. We promise, if you spend time with only those people on your Home team, you will perceive life better, feel better, and live life better.

Ask yourself if what you're doing today is getting you closer to where you want to be tomorrow.

Whoa That's Deep

Almost all people live each day out of routine and habit. We get up at the same time, eat at the same time, and go to work at the same time. But, it goes deeper than this. We also have habitual or automatic responses to questions and experiences. For example, we often say we are *fine*, when asked how we are, when in fact we *aren't* fine.

Habits are so ingrained in us that we brush our teeth, tie our shoes and do many things without thought. We use mental and muscle memory. The saying, "We are creatures of habit," is true, and while much of what we do out of habit is not damaging to us, there are habits we have learned that are keeping us depressed, anxious, insecure, angry, and stuck where we don't want to be.

In working through the other tools, you should have a better understanding of how you function. Hopefully, reading this book has caused you to view life differently and you are beginning to know how amazing you really are.

You've started exercising, journaling, and are more hopeful about your future.

Now, we want to go deeper into who you are and want you to become more passionate and purposeful in how you live and function every day.

186

We need to build on what you've done so far to make sure you achieve lasting change. We want to increase the odds of success that your tomorrow is beautiful and will be lived on your own terms. This is not a one-day process but is a daily process over time. It may feel a bit foreign in the beginning to how you live each day currently, but if you keep taking the steps outlined in this book, in time loving yourself every day, and living life how you've dreamed will become a habit that you don't have to think about.

To get there, you must learn about yourself, which requires you to question your behavior, your thoughts and your responses. For this to work you must above all else be brutally honest with yourself. You may not like the true answers to these questions, but these answers are only the starting point. They're not final. You'll have everything you need to change how you answer them in the future. As a matter of fact, the goal is to change the way you answer them forever.

Take Action

Open to a blank journal page and date it to track the progress you make. Write the questions and the answers down and revisit them in a month or so to see if the answers have changed. We are going to give you some starter questions to ask but in time you will have your own. The most important part is if you don't like the answer to a question, ask yourself how you can change it. Then, get moving and make it happen!

- What behaviors do I have that are detrimental to my wellbeing?
- What recurring fears do I have and are they rational?
- Are there relationships with people in my life that need to end because they are unhealthy?
- What unhealthy daily habits do I depend on?

I can't go back to yesterday, because I was a different person then. -Lewis Carroll

Eyes Forward

There is a beautiful point in a journey where you have gone too far and it's best to just keep going forward rather than turn around and go back because there isn't a benefit to doing so.

If you've taken the steps laid out in this book so far, you've become a healthier person. While the book talks about the tragedies of only two people, you've discovered your own and have begun to heal, thus changing your future.

You no longer live out of your past. It now serves as a reminder of who you don't want to be and how you will never again function.

I'm Just That Into Me is more than a story. It's the way we should all live. There is absolutely nothing wrong with loving yourself and putting yourself first. Doing so gives you the ability to really love those around you. It also teaches others that taking care of yourself first is our most important job in this life.

You only get to live today once so making it the best you can starts with you and your mental, emotional, and physical health. You can't neglect any of these and live a peaceful, joy-filled life. You are worthy of a happy and whole life. One where you and you alone, control your outcome. That's real freedom. This doesn't mean doing or saying whatever you want, but being intentional about what you need to do that leads to your best outcome.

Freedom is like finally hitting the road for a trip you've been waiting for. It's that feeling you get when you allow yourself to just be you and do what is good for you. This comes only when you are true to who you really are. When you love yourself enough to put you first. This sounds selfish and to some degree it is, but it's the healthiest way to live. When you put yourself first, it gives you the ability to be an amazing, mom, dad, husband, wife, or friend, because you have met your own needs. Therefore, you aren't relying on anyone else to make you feel loved. You will already feel loved. This completely frees you from the expectations you put on other people to be your source of happiness. From this point forward, all relationships are a bonus and not needed for survival.

We are designed to be our own hope, peace, joy and love. This process takes time and consistency, but we assure you a beautiful change that will alter the way you live and bring deeper more meaningful relationships with others and, more importantly, with yourself.

Take Action

The first part of this exercise is both easy and awkward. You will begin speaking to yourself in a way that is likely to be uncomfortable.

Sit or stand in front of a mirror and while looking in your eyes, speak words of love and encouragement to yourself, similar to what you would tell a child or anyone else you love.

Here are some examples of love and life-giving words you can say to yourself:

- o You're amazing.
- o You deserve happiness.
- o You deserve success.
- o You can reach your goals.
- o You are priceless.
- o You are precious.
- o You are talented and beautiful.
- o and any other great or loving things that are meaningful to you.

We accept love when believe we deserve it. If you set the bar low for how you treat yourself, then you will tolerate potentially damaging or terrible treatment from others. We implore you to stop this and love yourself.

The second part of this exercise is to counteract the negative thoughts in your head. As you're going about your day, anytime you have a negative thought, like, *I'm an idiot, I'm ugly, I'm worthless,* etc., counter the thought with a positive thought, like, *I'm smart, I'm beautiful, I'm priceless* or *I love me.*

The positive impact on your perception of yourself in doing this is truly amazing. The more you think and talk in a loving way to yourself, the more you will begin to see how much negativity is all around you every day and that negativity will affect you less and less. Give it a try, you won't regret it.

"The biggest adventure you can take is to live the life of your dreams."   *-Oprah Winfrey*

Dream a Little Dream

Children are amazing. No one has to tell them to smile, laugh, play or dream. They just do it and they do it with everything they have.

For them, it doesn't matter if they are poor or rich, what color they are, or if they are boys or girls. They are unencumbered by virtually anything. Nothing detours them from dreaming. They dream that someday they will be superheroes, actors, rock stars, astronauts and a million other things which seem unattainable to the adults in their midst. However, they fully believe it's possible.

So, what changes from childhood to adulthood to erase the part of us that dreams? The answer is nothing. Inside every living person there is a desire to do amazing things. To live a peaceful, joyful, life and to be who you are supposed to be.

The internet is littered with stories of people who started at the bottom and used their adversity to accomplish great things and become who they were meant to be. Everyone's story is different and beautiful, and the goal isn't to copy what someone else has done. That wouldn't bring you happiness.

Right now, *you* have the opportunity to write your own story and have your own extraordinary life. It started with your decision to read this book and take the steps laid out in it.

So, what do you do you dream about? What makes you smile when you think about it? Who do you want to be? Where do you want to go?

These are all the typical questions people ask, but there isn't anything typical about *your* answer. Your answers are precious and special to *you* and to the direction for your life.

Now is the time for you to pursue these things. You have everything you need to get started. The most important step is the first step and then the next step. In other words, you must decide it's time to start and then you must keep taking steps, even small steps, towards your dreams.

The difference between dreams and goals is a goal is a dream with a deadline. You give dreams life by setting a completion date and pursuing it at all costs. In the process, you must remember that you may fail or experience setbacks. This is just a normal part of the process. Everyone fails. Even Thomas Edison, inventor of the light bulb, failed, and he has been quoted as saying, "I have not failed. I've just found ten thousand ways that won't work."

You just can't quit. You have to keep going even if it is a struggle sometimes. Struggling is healthy. If we're struggling, we are still fighting to succeed. So, keep fighting for every dream and goal you have.

Take Action

It's time to take out the journal and write down a few dreams or goals that you have. Set both small, easy goals and big challenging ones. A small goal is easy to accomplish and can be done in a short time. It also gets you in the habit of succeeding, and we all need wins in our life. They fuel our passion and are encouraging, giving us a sense of accomplishment and a desire to keep dreaming.

Most people at some point have felt so defeated that they quit trying. This is avoidable with small goals. Bigger dreams take longer and the cost is higher, mentally, physically, and emotionally, but they also reap huge rewards. Some superhero dreams are bigger than we believe we're capable of. You'll have to grow into them, but don't give them up.

The process of pursuing goals changes us in many ways. They stretch us to the end of what we believe we are capable of, completely changing who we see in the mirror. So, dream and dream big. You are enough to accomplish your dreams. Don't let anything or anyone stand in the way of who you are supposed to be. We don't know you, but we know that you can love yourself enough to chase your dreams. Start small, but please start. Life is going to go by either way, so why not make it an amazing journey?

No one has ever regretted the pursuit of their dreams. Everyone regrets *not* pursuing their dreams.

The number one regret of the dying (from the book, *The Top Five Regrets of the Dying*) is ...

I wish I'd had the courage to live a life true to myself, not the life others expected of me.

Live a life without regrets. Love yourself and pursue your dreams. You're worth it exactly the way you are.